AIR WAR
over
Southeast Asia

A Pictorial Record
Vol. 3 1971-1975

By Lou Drendel

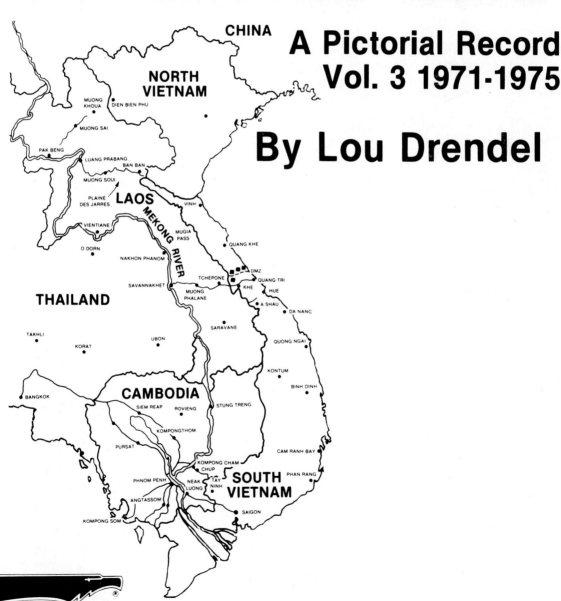

CHINA

NORTH VIETNAM

MUONG KHOUA

DIEN BIEN PHU

MUONG SAI

PAK BENG

LUANG PRABANG

BAN BAN

MUONG SOUI

PLAINE DES JARRES

LAOS

VINH

VIENTIANE

MUGIA PASS

O DORN

MEKONG RIVER

QUANG KHE

NAKHON PHANOM

DMZ

TCHEPONE

QUANG TRI

SAVANNAKHET

MUONG PHALANE

KHE

HUE

THAILAND

A SHAU

DA NANG

TAKHLI

SARAVANE

QUONG NGAI

KORAT

UBON

KONTUM

BINH DINH

CAMBODIA

STUNG TRENG

SIEM REAP

ROVIENG

BANGKOK

KOMPONGTHOM

PURSAT

CAM RANH BAY

KOMPONG CHAM

CHUP

PHAN RANG

PHNOM PENH

NEAK LUONG

TAY NINH

SOUTH VIETNAM

ANGTASSOM

SAIGON

KOMPONG SOM

squadron/signal publications

COPYRIGHT © 1984 SQUADRON/SIGNAL PUBLICATIONS, INC.

1115 CROWLEY DRIVE, CARROLLTON, TEXAS 75011-5010

ISBN 0-89747-148-2

If you have any photographs of the aircraft, armor, soldiers or ships of any nation, particularly wartime snapshots, why not share them with us and help make Squadron/Signal's books all the more interesting and complete in the future. Any photograph sent to us will be copied and the original returned. The donor will be fully credited for any photos used. Please indicate if you wish us not to return the photos. Please send them to: Squadron/Signal Publications, Inc., 1115 Crowley Dr., Carrollton, TX 75011-5010.

Photo Credits

USAF
US Navy
US Army
US Marine Corps
Norman E. Taylor
F. C Brown
Andy Mutzig
Wayne Mutza
Ron Verner
Ron Botz
Ron Lauer
Bob Baldo
Mike Lecroy
Ralph Hood
Neal Thompson

(Front Cover) A-7D SLUF (nee Corsair II) of the 354 TFW. The A-7, with its superior navigational and weapons delivery computers, took over and starred in the "Sandy" role during Linebacker II.

(Back Cover) Steve Ritchie got his third and fourth MiG 21s on 8 July, 1972. He flew over the top of the fireball created when his Sparrow missile blasted the first.

AIR WAR OVER SOUTHEAST ASIA 1971

As the American troop commitment in Vietnam wound down, North Vietnamese reliance on conventional warfare to conquer South Vietnam increased. The Viet Cong had ceased to be an effective political or military force with the stunning communist defeat suffered during the Tet Offensive of 1968. There was no longer any possibility of an indigenous guerilla force overthrowing the government of South Vietnam, simply because that force had ceased to exist in the carnage of the Tet Offensive. Any communist victory in the south would have to be achieved by the North Vietnamese regular Army, and the North proved exceptionally singleminded in this regard.

Contrary to what might have reasonably been expected, the avowed and demonstrated pull-out of American forces, coupled with undisguised North Vietnamese aggression, did not result in any diminution of the antiwar movement in the United States. The radical chic of the late sixties and early seventies demanded that any liberal who admitted to being liberal also must voice his unequivocal opposition to the American Government's policy in Vietnam. The antiwar movement had become unreasoning, intransigent, and blind to what was actually happening in Vietnam. Fortunately, Richard Nixon was not the sort of President who would allow his decisions to be swayed by this radical chic.

The North Vietnamese were marshalling their forces for an all-out spring offensive in 1971, after operations in Cambodia during the spring of 1970 had destroyed communist supply lines through that country into South Vietnam, aborting any communist offensive in 1970. Prior to the joint US-ARVN invasion of Cambodia, it was estimated that up to eighty-five percent of all communist materiel funneled through Cambodia, particularly through the port of Sihanoukville. When that supply line was closed, the communists were forced to rely upon the Ho Chi Minh Trail through Laos. By January of 1971, the Trail was nearly as busy as the LA Freeway at rush hour, and the North was obviously poised for a major invasion of the South. In order to secure their remaining invasion route, the North Vietnamese moved three divisions of troops into the Laotian panhandle, and emplaced dozens of SAMs and hundreds of AAA gunsites along the Trail.

Though nominally neutral, Laos was in fact a clandestine battleground. The North Vietnamese maintained an army of occupation of up to 100,000 troops, which assisted and controlled the Pathet Lao (the Laotion communists). They also maintained the Ho Chi Minh Trail through Laos. The Trail was a series of roads and pathways, able to accommodate anything from bicycle porters to tanks. It was the principal North Vietnamese invasion route to the south, and as such, received a considerable amount of attention from Allied air forces. The United States provided advisors and weaponry to the Laotion Government, and the American Central Intelligence Agency helped to maintain an army of 30,000 Meo tribesmen under Major General Vang Pao. This clandestine army, along with the CIA's own airline, Air America, maintained what was in effect an almost illusory American presence in Laos, which had little or no effect on North Vietnamese operations.

Intelligence reports that the North Vietnamese were on the verge of launching a major invasion of the south from their Laotion sanctuaries prompted President Nixon to authorize the same sort of operation that had been so successful the previous year in Cambodia. The American name for the operation was DEWEY CANYON II. But American participation was limited to aerial interdiction, close support, and tactical airlift. All of the grunts on the mission were ARVN, and for that reason the name which became public knowledge was LAM SON 719.

The attack into Laos was named after a Vietnamese victory over the Chinese in 1427, and got under way on February 8, 1971. The South Vietnamese general in charge was the commander of ARVN I Corps, Lieutenant General Hoang Xuan Lam. He chose some of South Vietnam's best troops, including the Airborne Division, Marine Brigade, 1st Infantry Division, and the 1st Armored Brigade to carry out the attacks on the Ho Chi Minh Trail. At 1000 hours on 8 February, 1971, over 5,000 ARVN troops crossed the frontier on highway 9, west of Khe Sanh, the former Marine combat base that served as the staging area for the attack. The plan was for the ground forces to link up with the airlifted troops around Tchepone, consolidate their positions, then seek out and destroy North Vietnamese supply dumps. Withdrawal from Laos was scheduled for March 10. As the invasion force advanced, ARVN Rangers and Airborne troops established fire bases on the peaks along route 9.

Total American forces involved in the operation were 10,000 men, 2,000 fixed-wing and 600 rotary-wing aircraft. US ground troops were restricted to operations within South Vietnam, which meant that their combat role was confined to the initial phase of the operation, consisting of the clearing of Highway 9, from Quang Tri to Khe Sanh. In spite of a news blackout, word of the impending attack leaked, and the North Vietnamese were denouncing expansion of the war into Laos by the United States even before the attack got under way. President Nixon, in his memoirs, stated that LAM SON 719 was a "military success, but a public relations disaster." The foundations for that disaster were laid immediately, as the American antiwar lobby joined Peking and Moscow in calling the forthcoming operation—"imperialist aggression".

The North Vietnamese counterattacked and many vicious battles were fought, with the ARVN troopers giving better than they got, though the advance towards Tchepone was bogged down by the heavy fighting. In an attempt to break the North Vietnamese defense, General Lam used 120 US Army Hueys to airlift two ARVN infantry battalions into the Tchepone area. In spite of the fact that the attack was preceded by B-52 strikes, and clear weather allowed maximum use of close air support, the helicopters encountered the heaviest anti-aircraft fire of the war. It is to their credit, and the discredit of the North Vietnamese gunners, that only one helicopter was lost. This final assault resulted in the achievement of most of the objectives of LAM SON 719. In a joint communique issued on 8 March, US and ARVN commands pronounced the operation an unqualified success. Large caches of weapons, ammunition, and foodstuffs had been captured or destroyed. Over 13,000 enemy had been killed, for the loss of 2,000 Allied soldiers. Enemy losses also included 76 artillery pieces, 106 tanks, 405 trucks, and 1,934 crew-served weapons.

The communist propaganda network was nothing, if not inventive. Their scoreboard for LAM SON 719 read as follows:

In more than 60 days and nights of fighting shoulder-to-shoulder with the Southern Lao population and liberation forces against the enemy's "LAM SON 719" operation, the population and armed forces at the Khe Sanh Front have recorded great victories. We have frustrated all US strategic schemes for its military adventure. We have destroyed an important part of the enemy forces and war means, including: nearly 7,000 troops, with 4,054 GIs wiped out, 863 military vehicles, including 236 tanks and armored personnel carriers gutted, 234 aircraft shot down or destroyed on the ground, 72 cannon and big mortars wrecked, 42 war vessels captured or burned, 41 big logistic bases and supply dumps containing millions of liters of fuel and thousands of tons of weapons, ammunition, food and military supplies, etc., destroyed.

Actual Allied losses were 115 aircraft, of which 107 were helicopters, 75 tanks, and 198 crew-served weapons. During 30 days of heavy fighting in

USS Enterprise crewmen prepare to launch a sunset mission. August of 1971 in the South China Sea. (US Navy)

In one of the last checks before launch, a catapult crewman checks the launch bridle cable on an A-3 Skywarrior. (US Navy)

EKA-3B launching from USS Coral Sea, 15 January, 1972, in the Gulf of Tonkin. The Skywarrior began life as a nuclear attack bomber, but by the time it received its baptism of fire over Vietnam, it was used exclusively in support roles such as reconnaissance, electronic countermeasures, and aerial refuelling. (US Navy)

Laos South Vietnamese forces had acquitted themselves well, standing up to numerically superior forces, even when weather prevented effective air support.

In anticipation of worsening weather, and feeling that most of the objectives of the operation had been met, General Lam ordered the withdrawal of his forces from Laos. The Assistant Division Commander of the 101st Airborne Division, Brigadier General Sidney B. Berry, Jr., ordered his pilots to load their helicopters to the absolute maximum in an effort to cut down on the number of sorties required to accomplish the withdrawal; an order that made good tactical sense in minimizing the exposure to the anti-aircraft fire of the North Vietnamese. Unfortunately this precipitated a disastrous image of the whole operation. Loading helicopters to the absolute limit often meant having ARVN troopers hanging on the skids. When photos of this were released by the wire services they painted a picture of withdrawal turned to rout. It was an undeserved epilogue to an operation in which the South Vietnamese had fought bravely and well. The major American media, never known for their dissemination of good news, quickly seized on these images and turned the withdrawal into a bug-out, ignoring the official versions of LAM SON 719. Headlines such as: "SCRAMBLE FOR SAFETY" and "The invasion of Laos comes to an end in bitter debate and a run for cover", heralded American reportage of the operation. As far as the American public (and to a large extent, the South Vietnamese public) was concerned, LAM SON 719 had been a complete disaster, reinforcing the opinion that the war was unwinnable.

The experts knew better. Sir Robert Thompson, the British expert on guerrilla warfare, wrote to Henry Kissinger from Vietnam after the operation, praising its military success. He also offered the opinion that the outcome of the war would now depend upon South Vietnamese psychology and confidence. His words were prophetically accurate. By any rational estimate, LAM SON 719 had been a tactical victory. In the strategic short run, it was also successful, forcing the North Vietnamese to again postpone their plans for a spring invasion for a full year, and reducing casualties within South Vietnam while the withdrawal of US forces continued. But like so much of the Vietnam War, the propaganda victory belonged to the communists, whose allies in the major western media turned a tactical victory into widespread doubt about the fighting abilities of ARVN.

Antiwar forces kept the brutality of the war in the forefront of the news with the conviction of Lieutenant William Calley in the My Lai Massacre. Though no one could condone Calley's actions in the premeditated murder of 22 South Vietnamese civilians, the general public was for clemency for Calley. His court martial sentenced him to life imprisonment at hard labor, but President Nixon, with the support of a majority of Congressional leaders, intervened, reducing the sentence to ten years. Calley was eventually paroled in 1974. There was little doubt in the minds of most Americans that Calley's actions were not representative of our efforts in the war, and even his actions were felt to be the result of the covert nature of the Viet Cong attacks suffered by his unit. However, the lurid reportage of the massacre,

highlighted by the gore of color photography, accentuated the horrors of the war. If the atrocities of the North Vietnamese and Viet Cong had received a fraction of the coverage My Lai got, there would have been no slackening of the will of the American public to support the objectives of the war. As it was, the media chose to ignore much of the brutality of the enemy. If one relied upon the television networks or the major print media for information on the conduct of the war, you would have believed that the communists were pure-of-heart revolutionaries, while the United States was only interested in brutally defending a way of life that was manifestly corrupt. Fortunately, much of the major media was looked upon with some distrust by a majority of Americans, and the media's increasingly antiwar bias only served to alienate generations that had grown up trusting their news media.

The Laotion invasion and the Calley trial were not the only Vietnam problems faced by the Nixon Administration in 1971. In June the Pentagon Papers story broke. The Pentagon Papers were a 7,000-page study of American involvement in Vietnam from World War II through 1968, commissioned by Robert McNamara. Officially titled, "The History of US Decision-Making Process on Vietnam", the study had been compiled from information contributed by the Department of Defense, the State Department, and the Central Intelligence Agency. Many verbatim documents were included in the study, and much of it was classified as SECRET or TOP SECRET. Though the Pentagon Papers primarily discredited the manner in which the Kennedy and Johnson Administrations conducted Vietnam Policy, their release would compromise intelligence sources still in place. They would also cause a good deal of political embarrassment among foreign leaders if their communications with the American Government were publicized. This would result in less-than-candid exchanges in the future. Under the circumstances, the Nixon Administration concluded that the prudent course to follow would be to attempt to block publication through court injunction.

The New York Times had gained access to the study when it was passed to them illegally by a former Pentagon employee, Daniel Ellsberg. Ellsberg's action was at best that of a common thief, and at worst that of a traitor. He was lionized by the media. The New York Times and Washington Post in particular betrayed their First Amendment trust by demonstrating double standards when it came to the Vietnam War. Though the Pentagon Papers would obviously damage the US, and in spite of the fact that they were obtained illegally, both of these newspapers allowed their antiwar bias to guide their policies. And the US Supreme Court showed somewhat less-than-supreme good judgment by allowing their publication. It was one more indication that many Americans did not have the patience or fortitude to support a war that would probably continue with or without US participation. America was getting out of Vietnam.

A-6 Intruder of VA-165 enroute to targets in North Vietnam on 5 May, 1972. (US Navy)

VA-165 Intruder has just been hauled to a stop by the arresting cable aboard USS Constellation after an April, 1972, mission over Vietnam. (US Navy)

A-7E of VA-192 "Golden Dragons" off the USS Kitty Hawk on a 1971 mission over Vietnam. With its state-of-the-art weapons delivery computers, the Corsair II made its pilots the best bombers in the fleet. (LTV)

VFP-63 RF-8G operated from the USS Midway in 1971. (Shinichi Ohtaki)

(Left) The RF-8 Crusader was the primary naval reconnaissance aircraft throughout the Vietnam War. This RF-8 is taxiing to a forward cat aboard USS Coral Sea.

KA-6D tanker refuelling VF-92 "Silver Kings" Phantoms prior to ingress on a 1971 combat mission. The tanker version of the Intruder could carry up to 3,844 gallons of fuel, of which 3,000 were transferable at rates of up to 350 gallons per minute. (US Navy)

A-7s of VA-27 "Royal Maces" overfly the USS Constellation in the Gulf of Tonkin. (US Navy)

(Above Right) USS Constellation underway in the South China Sea during a 1974 deployment to WestPac. (US Navy)

USS Hancock in the Gulf of Tonkin 25 May, 1972. Hancock was one of five attack carriers operating in the Gulf during the spring of 1972. Saratoga, Midway, Constellation, and Kitty Hawk also sent their air wings against North Vietnam in response to the Easter Invasion of South Vietnam. (US Navy)

A-7E of VA-146 "Blue Diamonds" being positioned on the catapult aboard USS Constellation prior to a 25 April, 1972, mission against North Vietnam. (US Navy)

A-7s of VA-27 and an A-6 of VA-196 aboard Connie being made ready to depart on a mission over North Vietnam in 1972.

"Blue Diamonds" A-7 returning to USS America after a 1970 mission over Vietnam. (US Navy)

1972

Except for LAM SON 719, there were no major military operations during 1971. Negotiations remained deadlocked, with the North Vietnamese convinced that the US would leave Vietnam at all costs, and that there was little to be gained by negotiating concessions to the existence of a US-backed government in the south. But while they had unquestionably scored a propaganda victory in LAM SON 719, the communists realized that ARVN was gaining in competency, and if Vietnamization was allowed to continue unchallenged, the south might prove capable of defending itself without US troops. Clearly, it was to the advantage of the North to invade the South as soon as possible. If they were able to inflict heavy US casualties in the process, so much the better, since that would probably only hasten the American withdrawal.

By February of 1972 the North Vietnamese had moved their thirteen mainforce divisions into position for a spring offensive in the south. Five were in Laos, seven were in South Vietnam, and the one remaining in North Vietnam was poised at the DMZ. New SAM and AAA sites had been built in Laos and in the lower panhandle of North Vietnam. Heavy artillery had been emplaced just north of the DMZ, new roads had been constructed through the DMZ into South Vietnam, two new airfields had been built in southern North Vietnam, and tons of supplies had been positioned for the upcoming assault. All of this activity was well documented by Allied intelligence. Contrary to 1970 and 1971, when spoiling attacks had aborted North Vietnamese invasions of the south, the communist preparations for this all-out attack were allowed to go on unmolested.

While the North Vietnamese were busily preparing to invade the south, Richard Nixon was in communist China, telling Chou En Lai that his requirement for complete withdrawal of Americans from South Vietnam was a negotiated cease-fire and a return of all American POWs. This, he said, had been offered to the North Vietnamese, who had rejected these terms, insisting that the United States impose a political settlement on the South Vietnamese which would give the communists an active role in the government of the south. Chou urged Nixon to withdraw as quickly as he could, warning him that the North Vietnamese would never surrender. Nixon replied that the United States could never abandon its friends in that manner, since such an action would demonstrate to friend and foe alike that the United States was unreliable in its commitments. The result of the Nixon trip to China was the Shanghai Communique, which pledged in part that neither nation "should seek hegemony in the Asia Pacific region and each is opposed to efforts by any other country or group of countries to establish such hegemony." It was Nixon's view that this was a thinly disguised warning to the Russians by the Chinese. It could just as well have been meant for the North Vietnamese, whose appetite for conquest was soon to be demonstrated.

Early in 1972 it became evident that the North Vietnamese were not going to negotiate anything. Therefore, President Nixon decided to go public with the details of the, until then, secret negotiations taking place in Paris. He included details of an American proposal which the North Vietnamese would not even listen to. It was by far the most conciliatory offer to date, and included withdrawal of all American troops within six months of a cease-fire, which would include all of Indochina, and an internationally supervised presidential election in the south. South Vietnamese President Thieu and Vice

President Ky had even agreed to resign a month before this election would take place! Nixon also revealed the details of the North Vietnamese propaganda coup in which they had so adroitly maneuvered George McGovern into publicly proposing a peace plan which would be "acceptable" to them. They didn't reveal that it was a plan which had been proposed by Kissinger months before in the secret negotiations, and which they had turned down. When confronted with this, the North Vietnamese negotiator, Xuan Thuy said, "What Senator McGovern says is his problem." In his 25 January speech, Nixon also stated his willingness to consider any reasonable peace plan. But he warned that he would not allow hostile action to endanger the lives of the 69,000 Americans remaining in South Vietnam.

The South Vietnamese, realizing that they would have to bear the brunt of the upcoming invasion, accelerated their training programs and cancelled all leaves. They were as ready as they could be when the communists struck. Ceilings and visibilities were severely restricted by low, scudding monsoon rain clouds when the communists attacked across the DMZ and into Quang Tri Province on 30 March, 1972. It was the beginning of what came to be known as the Easter Offensive. For the first time in the war the NVA employed tanks in massed formations. This was the conventional warfare that Allied tacticians had tried for years to lure the communists into fighting. The attacks across the DMZ were coordinated with similar attacks from Laos and Cambodia against Pleiku and An Loc.

The initial attacks were met with stiff resistance by ARVN, but without the close air support which was denied by weather, they were slowly worn down by the weight of the NVA onslaught, and forced to fall back and regroup. It was evident that airpower would have to play a pivotal role if the invasion was to be blunted.

B-52 ARC LIGHT strikes were flown against the NVA INVASION FORCES, using radar bombing techniques, and as the weather slowly improved, more and more tactical airpower was brought to bear on the North Vietnamese. More B-52s were ordered to Southeast Asia, and by late June the B-52 force numbered 200 bombers, flying up to 3,150 sorties per month. In a move designed to demonstrate his determination to prevent a North Vietnamese victory in the south, President Nixon ordered the B-52s into the Hanoi-Haiphong area for the first time in the war. On 21 and 23 April the BUFs struck Bai Thuong Airfield, Vinh, Thanh Hoa, the Haiphong Petroleum Products storage area, and Hamn Rong transshipment point, in OPERATION FREEDOM PORCH BRAVO. It was hoped that these attacks would give the North Vietnamese something to think about, and perhaps inspire serious negotiations. (Prior to this, Henry Kissinger had been assured by Russian Ambassador Anatoly Dobrynin that the North Vietnamese would assume a much more flexible posture when the "secret" talks resumed in Paris on April 24. Since the Russians were the principal sponsors of the North Vietnamese, there was every reason to believe there might be progress. Then, when the North Vietnamese cancelled the 24 April meeting, the Russians denied that they had any influence on NVA plans, or that they had supplied much in the way of weaponry!

The summit meeting with the Soviets was on the horizon, and President

VA-147 "Argonauts" operated their A-7s off Constellation during the spring 1972 campaign against North Vietnam. (US Navy)

VA-56 "Champions" A-7Bs enroute to targets in March, 1973. (US Navy)

The time-honored custom of decorating aircraft which land on the wrong carrier with graffiti was carried on during the Vietnam War. This VA-195 Corsair II landed aboard Coral Sea instead of its home carrier Kitty Hawk and paid the price. 26 April, 1972. (US Navy)

A-6A Intruder of VMA-224 aboard Coral Sea prior to 7 May, 1972, mission. It is loaded with Mk 20 Rockeye anti-armor cluster bombs. The Rockeye incorporated 96 shaped-charge bomblets, stacked around a Zuni rocket motor which dispersed them after release. It was effective against hard targets. (US Navy)

Pilot and Bombardier-Navigator prepare to board their VA-165 Intruder prior to a May, 1972, mission against North Vietnam. (US Navy)

Nixon wanted Kissinger, in his preparatory talks with the Soviets, to stress that anything else the Russians might be interested in negotiating would depend upon their using their influence to end the war in Vietnam. Kissinger wanted to be more flexible in his dealings with the Russians, and pointed out to the President that even if the North Vietnamese should win the war he would still be hailed on the home front for withdrawing.

Nixon, in a flash of insight which demonstrated his expertise in foreign affairs, replied, "I don't give a damn about the domestic reaction if that happens, because if it does, sitting in this office wouldn't be worth it. The foreign policy of the United States will have been destroyed, and the Soviets will have established that they can accomplish what they are after by using the force of arms in third countries. Defeat is simply not an option!" In the end, Nixon allowed Kissinger to set the agenda for a Nixon-Brezhnev summit without insisting upon a Vietnam settlement as a prerequisite. The summit was arranged during Kissinger's trip to Moscow that spring, but Nixon demonstrated that he was not letting the Russians off the hook entirely with a tough speech two days after Kissinger's return. In that speech, the President described the North Vietnamese attack by saying, "There is only one word for it...INVASION." He promised that the bombing of North Vietnam would continue until their military offensive had stopped. The North Vietnamese demonstrated that they understood this kind of language by rescheduling the cancelled 24 April meeting for 2 May.

The President's instructions to Kissinger for this meeting were tough and to the point, "...they have violated all understandings, they have stepped up the war, they have refused to negotiate seriously. The President has had enough and now you have only one message to give them, 'Settle or else!'" But the North Vietnamese were insulting and unresponsive during the meeting with Kissinger, and after three hours, the meeting broke up without any positive results.

A-4s from Hancock knocked down the Duong Phuong Thuong bridge in North Vietnam during April of 1972. (US Navy)

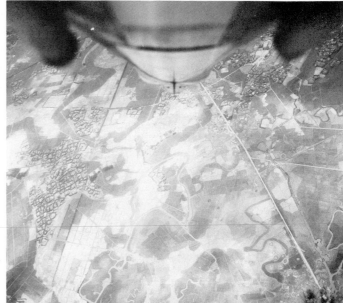

VA-165 Intruders overfly Constellation as an A-7 crosses the fantail recovering from a mission over the North in May of 1972. (US Navy)

(Above Right) A-4F of CVW-21 pulls out after scoring a direct hit on the Son Trieu highway bridge (lower right) in North Vietnam during April of 1972. (US Navy)

(Right) A-6 loaded with three and one half tons of bombs enroute to North Vietnam in May, 1972. (US Navy)

In the meantime, events on the battlefield had taken a turn for the worse. The communists had captured Quang Tri and, though it was not considered militarily vital by US experts, the effect on South Vietnamese morale was devastating. As the battle for Hue—a city that was considered militarily vital—began, it was clear that the United States would have to do something to shore up South Vietnamese resolve, and send a message to the North Vietnamese and their Russian sponsors that their aggression would not succeed. The question was, what could the United States do that would achieve these goals, while preserving the upcoming summit and the much-ballyhooed "detente" with the Russians?

F-4B of VF-111 being hooked to the cat aboard Coral Sea prior to 10 April, 1972, mission against North Vietnam. (US Navy)

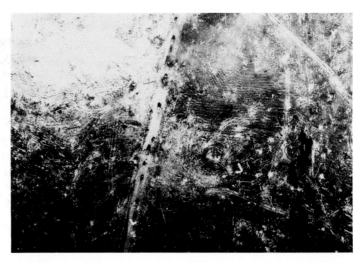

On 23 April, 1972, A-7s from VA-146 flying from USS Constellation caught this NVA convoy north of the city of An Loc. They destroyed most of the Soviet-made URAL-375 trucks. Though surrounded and outnumbered, ARVN, with around-the-clock air support, held An Loc. (US Navy)

EKA-3B at Danang in September, 1972. Danang was one of the primary divert fields for carrier-based aircraft. (Andy L. Mutzig)

RF-8G of VFP-63, escorted by an F-8J of VF-211, preparing to recover aboard Hancock after an April, 1973, mission. (US Navy)

LINEBACKER I

USS America-based A-7s of VA-86 join with VF-161 Phantoms off the Midway for a Loran bombing mission in March of 1973. (US Navy)

F-4D Phantom from the 13th TFS equipped with Loran navigational equipment provides bomb release commands for a pair of VF-151 F-4Bs during a March, 1973, mission. (US Navy)

What the President decided to do was what military experts had been saying should have been being done since the beginning of the war. In his own words, "The only way to stop the killing is to take the weapons of war out of the hands of the international outlaws of North Vietnam." To that end he decided that air operations (and this time, effective air operations) against North Vietnam would have to be reinstituted. His advisors were split on the wisdom of this. Secretary of Defense Melvin Laird was against it, while Secretary of State Rodgers indicated that he would be for it if it worked. Kissinger noted that, even if we lost in Vietnam Nixon would still be given credit for withdrawing. Almost all of them felt that the Russians would cancel the summit if Nixon went ahead with concentrated and effective bombing of the North. But the President noted that "The summit isn't worth a damn if the price for it is losing in Vietnam. My instinct tells me that the country can take losing the summit, but it can't take losing the war." John Connally, a member of the National Security Council, put the fear of Russian cancellation of the summit into proper perspective when he said, "...if they cancel, and I don't think they will, we'll ram it right down their throats."

On 8 May, 1972, the President went on television to announce that the communists had not only refused to consider his peace proposals, but had also failed to put forth counter-proposals. Under these circumstances, he had no other choice than to use other means to get their attention. He announced that he was: (1) mining all entrances to North Vietnamese ports to prevent access to these ports as well as all North Vietnamese naval operations from these ports; (2) US forces will take appropriate measures within the internal and claimed territorial waters of North Vietnam to interdict the delivery of any supplies; (3) rail and all other communications would be cut off to the maximum extent possible and that air and naval strikes against military targets in North Vietnam would be reinstituted. Domestic reaction to this speech was swift and predictable. The Democrats howled in outrage, introducing measures in Congress to limit the President's war-making powers. It was the unanimous opinion of the major media that the upcoming summit with the Russians would be postponed indefinitely. They were wrong. The Russians understood the language Nixon was speaking, and though they officially protested the renewed bombing, no mention was made of the summit. When Kissinger questioned Soviet Ambassador Dobrynin, in a circumspect manner, Dobrynin replied, "You have handled a difficult situation uncommonly well."

Rather than give the President credit for his courage and insight, the media attacked the bombing campaign, repeating and attempting to legitimize the propaganda coming from Hanoi. The chief propaganda claim had to do with the bombing of dikes in North Vietnam. Over several centuries the North Vietnamese had developed a system of 2500 miles of earthen dikes to control the annual flooding caused by monsoon rains. The monsoon of 1971 was especially heavy, and the majority of North Vietnamese were preoccupied with war-related duties. As a consequence, the dikes were not maintained and flooding occurred. The 1972 flooding had the potential for even worse results, since repair work on the dikes was postponed in favor of preparing for the invasion of South Vietnam. Though the dikes would have been legitimate targets under the law of war, their attack was never seriously considered at any time during the war. Even when the North Vietnamese began emplacing AAA and SAM sites on or near dikes, they remained off-limits to American bombers.

Ironically, it was not the media or the North Vietnamese who posed the greatest threat of failure in the new campaign, which had been dubbed OPERATION LINEBACKER. The Pentagon, after years of inept, ineffectual, and empty military threats and actions instituted by the Johnson Administration, was apparently not prepared for a President who had the guts to back up words with actions. The plan they advanced for LINEBACKER did not begin to match the "go-for-broke" mood of the President. He let them know, in no uncertain terms, that, having taken the political heat for the decision to step up pressures on North Vietnam, he was not going to be satisfied with halfway measures. The stupid and dangerous rules of engagement as propagated by the Johnson Administration went out the window. As Nixon noted in a memo to Kissinger: "I want the military to get off its backside...We have the power to destroy the enemy war-making capacity. The only question is whether we have the will to use that power. What distinguishes me from Johnson is that I have the will in spades!"

LINEBACKER I commenced with OPERATION POCKET MONEY, the mining of North Vietnamese ports. The mines were sown by Navy A-6s on 9 May. They were set for activation at 1800 hours on 11 May, giving the 16 Soviet, 5 Communist Chinese, 2 Cuban, 1 East German, 2 Polish, 5 Somali, and 5 British Hong Kong registered ships time to pull out; only five did. Since up to eighty-five percent of all imports had arrived through the port of Haiphong during 1971, including all OIL, this was a devastatingly effective blockade.

In addition, other vital supply lines were targeted, including the northeast and northwest rail lines, and the eight major highways leading into China. With supply lines cut, USAF, Navy, and Marine Corps aircraft set out to destroy the considerable stockpiles of weaponry within North Vietnam. They accomplished this to a degree that was impossible during the Rolling Thunder campaigns of 1965-68. Their success was due in part to precision-guided munitions, including laser and electro-optically guided bombs, which were immediately dubbed "smart bombs", as opposed to "dumb bombs", which received no guidance once they were released from the aircraft. Targets which had been virtually immune during Rolling Thunder, either because of the fear of casualties among civilians, or because of operational difficulties, were successfully struck. The Thanh Hoa bridge over the Song Ma River, long considered a major choke point for southbound supplies, was one of the first targets hit. "The Dragon's Jaw", as the bridge was called by the Vietnamese, had been the target of literally hundreds of sorties during Rolling Thunder. It had never been dropped until fourteen USAF F-4s attacked it with Mk 84 and Mk 113 Laser-Guided Bombs on 13 May.

The Soviet-built Lang Chi hydroelectric plant, located 63 miles northwest of Hanoi on the Red River, was capable of supplying up to seventy-five percent of Hanoi's electricity, but breaching its dam could drown up to 23,000 North Vietnamese civilians. On 10 June F-4 laser bombers put 12 Mk 84s through the 50x100-foot roof of the main building, destroying the plant's turbines and generators without putting a crack in the dam.

While field commanders were given much more latitude in attacking targets on the validated Joint Chiefs of Staff list, there were still restrictions. Gia Lam airport, the Hanoi thermal power plant, Hanoi international radio communications system, the Lao Dong Party headquarters (North Vietnamese equivalent of the Pentagon), the Ministry of Defense Army and Area

F-4J of VF-143 milliseconds away from launch aboard USS Enterprise on a 1972 MIGCAP mission.

F-4J of VF-21 about to plug into an A-3 tanker over the Gulf of Tonkin on a March, 1973, mission. (Jan Jacobs via Jim Sullivan)

The C-1A Trader was used throughout the war in the COD (Carrier On board Delivery) role. "Triple Nuts" was attached to USS Constellation in 1974. (US Navy)

RA-5C Vigilante of RVAH-5, "The Savage Sons of Sanford" over the South China Sea on an August, 1974, mission. RVAH-5 was the first squadron to fly the RA-5C, converting in 1964. The RA-5C provided reconnaissance for air groups on the larger carriers. (US Navy)

Helicopter Mine Countermeasures Squadron Twelve (HM-12) CH-53A pulling a magnetic orange pipe from the stern of the Amphibious Transport Dock USS Vancouver (LPD-2) during END SWEEP.

Marine Corps CH-53A sweeping Haiphong Harbor for mines during OPERATION END SWEEP, the May, 1973, operation to clear North Vietnamese harbors of the mines that were dropped at the beginning of LINEBACKER I. (US Navy)

Capital Headquarters, which was located in heavily populated central Hanoi, and economic targets not directly related to the military effort, including the Haiphong docks, were off-limits to the bombers. In addition, no strikes were made in the Hanoi-Haiphong area during President Nixon's visit to Moscow for the Summit Meeting, 21 May to 5 June, nor during Russian President Podgorny's visit to Hanoi in mid-June. This visit was as a result of a meeting between Nixon and Brezhnev during the Moscow summit. After initially threatening the introduction of foreign troops to aid North Vietnam, and having had that bluff called by Nixon, the Russians had gradually accepted the final position of the United States on the SALT treaty, and had hinted that they would use their influence with the North Vietnamese to get negotiations started again.

LINEBACKER continued throughout the summer and early fall of 1972. In September OPERATION PRIME CHOKE attacked the railroad bridges in the buffer zone between North Vietnam and China. Accuracy of PGM allowed strikes in what were previously considered to be sensitive areas. The laser bombers were so effective, in fact, that by the first of October it had become evident even to the zealots in Hanoi that they could not win the war

militarily. The Paris negotiations took on a new character, with the North Vietnamese apparently willing to bargain seriously for peace. As the talks began to appear fruitful, the bombing campaign gradually slackened, with restrictions on bombing the Hanoi-Haiphong area once again being instituted. This was followed, over the objections of General Fred C. Weyand (COMUSMACV), by a halt to all air operations above the 20th parallel on 23 October. It was on this date that Kissinger made his famous "Peace is at hand" remark.

While there was no bombing above the 20th parallel, interdiction of supply lines continued in southern North Vietnam. It was a mistake to show any mercy to the leaders of North Vietnam. Once the bombing had stopped, they reverted to their stalling tactics during the negotiations, while repairing their rail and highway links, and adding new stockpiles of offensive weaponry. In order to protect this replenished arsenal, they doubled the air defenses around Hanoi and Haiphong. It was going to take one more bombing campaign to convince the North Vietnamese that they could not win the war as long as Richard Nixon was in the White House.

A-7E of VA-27 launching from USS Enterprise on 29 April, 1975, to provide cover for the evacuation of Saigon. (US Navy)

Crusader's main gear has left the deck as the arresting gear yanks it to a halt aboard the Oriskany. (US Navy)

KA-6D of VA-165 and a tanker configured A-7E of VA-146 over the South China Sea in September, 1974. (US Navy)

(Below) A-6s of VA-145 flew the last bombing mission of the Vietnam War in 1975, using radar offset target identification. (US Navy)

The carriers operating in the South China Sea in 1975 often launched their aircraft without ordnance. An A-6 of VA-196 and an F-4B of VMFA-115 are about to launch from Enterprise on 15 January, 1975. (US Navy)

(Left) CH-46 and CH-53 were operated by Marine HMM 164 and HMM 463 respectively during early 1973.

VMFA-115 Phantom approaches Enterprise for a trap, while another is directed to one of the forward catapults for launch during cyclic operations in the South China Sea. (US Navy)

F-4J of VF-213 "Black Lions" about to be launched from USS Kitty Hawk in the South China Sea in February, 1976. (US Navy)

The Salvage Ship USS Safeguard (ARS-25) recovered the tail section of a Marine Corps CH-53 that crashed into Haiphong Harbor during END SWEEP. (US Navy)

(Left) A-6s of VMA(AW)-224 overfly the Coral Sea during air ops in the Gulf of Tonkin on 8 March, 1972. (US Navy)

(Below) VMCJ-1 operated the EA-6A from Danang on a TDY basis from their home base at Subic in the Philippines. They were particularly effective in jamming North Vietnamese SAM guidance radar during the big B-52 raids of LINEBACKER II. (Shinichi Ohtaki)

(Above) On 26 June, 1973, this CH-53 of HMM-165 encountered gear problems while approaching USS Tripoli for landing in Haiphong Harbor. The pilot brought the aircraft to a hover over the deck and allowed deck crewmen to hand-activate the gear before making a safe landing. (US Navy)

A pair of Chu Lai-based A-4Fs approach MCAS Iwakuni for a formation landing. (Shinichi Ohtaki)

A-6A of VMA(AW)-533 loaded for action against the North Vietnamese army during the spring, 1972, invasion. It carries Rockeye anti-armor bombs and 500-lb. bombs with fuze extenders to ensure that the bombs exploded above ground for maximum anti-personnel effect. (John Santucci)

NEGOTIATIONS

F-4B of VMFA-115 loaded with 2.75 rocket pods for a 1971 mission against the Viet Cong. (John Santucci)

As the aerial interdiction of military supplies in North Vietnam continued, and the North Vietnamese army suffered defeat after defeat on the battlefields of South Vietnam, a negotiated settlement of the war began to look more attractive to the communists. By August of 1972 they were apparently convinced that their last hope for victory in the south, namely, the election of George McGovern, was not going to happen. Once they were convinced that Richard Nixon would be reelected, they decided that better terms would be available before the election.

During negotiations in Paris in early October, Kissinger and Le Duc Tho achieved a basic understanding. The North Vietnamese dropped most of their formerly unreasonable demands and in the words of the President, "virtually capitulated". When Kissinger returned to Washington in mid-October, it was to brief the President on the details of what now seemed a sure thing. As a sign of good faith, the President ordered the Pentagon to reduce sorties over the north, but he would not halt bombing completely, feeling that the North Vietnamese had demonstrated too often in the past that they quickly forgot the meaning of good faith without military pressure to focus their attention. The only nagging worries about the agreements, which were scheduled to be signed in Paris on 30 October, were how President Thieu of South Vietnam would react to them. After all, he had no role in their negotiation, and could be expected to harbor no illusions about the honesty of the North Vietnamese.

The South Vietnamese delegation was less than enthusiastic about the agreements, which called for complete withdrawal of American forces from South Vietnam. The United States would be allowed to replace worn-out equipment on a one-for-one basis. Since the North Vietnamese continued to insist that they had no troops in South Vietnam, the agreements could not call for their withdrawal, but the agreements did specify the closing of logistical support bases in Cambodia and Laos, under international supervision. This would have the effect of starving the North Vietnamese army if it didn't return to North Vietnam. In spite of their haggling over details in the final draft, there was no hiding the fact that the North had lost the war, and the South was immeasurably stronger than it had been in the dark days of 1964-65. Still, the South Vietnamese were reluctant to see their American protectors go, feeling (quite accurately, as it turned out) that the communists would ignore any agreement to the extent possible without incurring retaliation by the United States. The North Vietnamese, ever the masters of propaganda, twisted and turned on the hook of a peace settlement, changing wording here, complaining that the United States was not expediting the process there, and all the while trying to drive a wedge between the United States and South Vietnam. Henry Kissinger's considerable skills as a

A-4F of VMA-311 rolls in on a bomb run against targets in I Corps area of South Vietnam on 27 February, 1971. It is armed with Snakeye bombs and napalm. (USMC)

negotiator were tested to the extreme trying to keep the North Vietnamese on the hook while he worked on Thieu.

The North Vietnamese attempted to turn defeat into victory by pressuring the United States to sign without the concurrence of Thieu by going public with the provisions of the agreements, including the original date for signing of the agreements. The North Vietnamese broadcast was what prompted Kissinger's press conference of 26 October, in which he stated, "We believe peace is at hand." He also stated that there were still salient points to be negotiated, but that these could probably be worked out in three or four sessions. But "peace is at hand" was just too good a lead-in to be tempered with any substantive doubts about the long-hoped-for end of the Vietnam War. The President refused to be stampeded into signing any agreement precipitously. While warning Thieu that obstructionism would erode the support of the American people for South Vietnam, he publicly stated that he would not sign any agreement until it was the right agreement, and would not hesitate one minute to sign the right agreement. As was the case with Nixon's first big military action in Southeast Asia, the Cambodian incursion of 1970, public support for LINEBACKER had been overwhelming, and Nixon's handling of the war was generally accepted as a strong plus for him in pre-election polls.

The North Vietnamese reverted to intransigence, insisting upon the original signing date. The President then authorized resumption of B-52 strikes over the north, beginning near the DMZ and moving northward daily. The communists quickly got the message, and scheduled new talks in Paris on 14 November. It was considered absolutely essential that Thieu be prepared to agree to the terms of the agreement when the time came, and in order to allay his fears about the agreements, President Nixon sent Kissinger's aide, Alexander Haig, whom Thieu liked personally, to Saigon. Haig carried a letter from Nixon to Thieu in which Nixon gave Thieu the following assurances: "You have my absolute assurance that if Hanoi fails to abide by the terms of this agreement it is my intention to take swift and severe retaliatory action." Thieu was apparently convinced to go along, with the stipulation that the DMZ be treated as a secure border, that the "non-existent" North Vietnamese troops be withdrawn from the South, and that Viet Cong participation in a coalition government not be a part of the agreement.

With the American election over, the North Vietnamese again seemed willing to stall in the hopes of exploiting Thieu's reluctance to accept an agreement. They actually retreated from some of the understandings of early October, prompting President Nixon to warn them that he was ready to resume military operations above the 20th parallel if they refused to negotiate seriously. But the communists had heard plenty of threats during the course of twenty-five years of fighting, and threats alone would not cause them to soften their position. The question was, could the administration rally the American People behind another major effort, after telling them that "peace was at hand"? Kissinger favored having the President go on television again, explaining that the North Vietnamese had brought the talks to a halt with unreasonable demands, and that it had become necessary to resume heavy bombing above the 20th parallel. The President, on the other hand, felt that if it was necessary to resume heavy bombing, the less said the better. Those on the receiving end would be no less affected for the lack of public explanations for its necessity. But before resorting to renewed bombing, the President pressured the Soviets and the Communist Chinese to lean on the North Vietnamese. While this pressure resulted in less arrogance at the negotiating table, there was still no movement in the North Vietnamese positions.

On 13 December Le Duc Tho put an end to the talks, announcing that he intended to leave for Hanoi the following day for consultations. Kissinger's assessment of the North Vietnamese, as quoted in President Nixon's memoirs, was: "They're just a bunch of shits. Tawdry, filthy shits. They make the Russians look good, compared to the way the Russians make the Chinese look good when it comes to negotiating in a responsible and decent way!" There now seemed no other option than to resume bombing. But this time, President Nixon demonstrated what he meant when he said he had "the will in spades". Rather than resume bombing with tactical aircraft alone, which would be severely restricted because of poor weather in the Hanoi-Haiphong area, the President decided to hit the North Vietnamese hard. And that meant B-52s.

Lt. Bob Ludwig flew "Li'l Cheryl" during 44th TFS operations against targets in Laos and Cambodia. (USAF)

This F-105F limped back to Takhli, but was considered irreparable and was relegated to the boneyard, where it was cannibalized for parts. (B/G Don Kutyna)

(Left) F-4Ds of the 8th TFW prepare to take off on a mission from Ubon RTAB. They are equipped with LORAN (note antenna on fuselage spine) which enabled them to bomb accurately through solid overcast. (USAF)

C-141A of the 63rd MAW based at Norton AFB, California, taxies at Danang on 16 February, 1971. It would later be the first C-141 to land in Hanoi to pick up POWs in 1973. (Norman E. Taylor)

Captain J. L. Hubbard preflights Mk 82 bombs loaded on the inboard pylons of his F-4 of the 389th TFS prior to an 8 October, 1971, mission from Phu Cat AB. (USAF)

(Above Right) OV-10A Bronco starting engines prior to a mission from Ubon RTAB on 20 April, 1971. The speed, range, and armament-carrying capability made the Bronco the USAF's ultimate Forward Air Controller (FAC) aircraft during the latter stages of the war. (USAF)

(Right) EC-47 of the 360th Tactical Electronic Warfare Squadron. EC-47s were used to locate enemy troop concentrations by intercepting radio transmissions. They provided much of the targeting information for tactical bombers, including B-52s. (USAF)

Pave Sword pod mounted under the Sparrow missile well. This pod was a laser seeker which was slaved to the F-4s radar. The laser designator was normally carried by an O2-A FAC. This combination allowed the F-4 to deliver the mystical "smart" bombs which devastated the NVA. (USAF)

F-4D of the 432nd TRW with ECM pods and special Pave pod on the centerline during a mission from Udorn in September, 1971. (USAF)

A-1E of the 56th SOW loaded with rocket pods, CBUs and minigun pods for rescue escort mission. (Al Piccirillo via Norman E. Taylor)

(Right) Air Base Security at Nakhon Phanom was provided by the 56th Security Police Squadron. Amn. Ricky L. Price patrolled the flightline with Thor, a German Shepherd sentry dog. October, 1972. (USAF)

"BALLS A FIRE" was flown by 1/Lt. Dale P. Townsend from Nakhon Phanom AB as a Sandy escort for Jolly Green Giant rescue helicopters. (USAF)

THE 1972 PRESIDENTIAL CAMPAIGN

Richard Nixon's detractors (and they have been legion) accused the President of orchestrating the peace negotiations in order to maximize his chances in the election. While Henry Kissinger was announcing that "Peace is at hand", the North Vietnamese were in fact preparing to teach Doctor Kissinger a lesson about their trustworthiness. Whether or not a peace of any kind in Vietnam was signed before or after the election would have made little difference to the outcome of the election. The fact of the matter was, the Democrats had nominated a candidate who could not get elected. Perhaps the only people in the country who did not think that George McGovern was a Radical-Liberal was the eastern establishment media, and a majority of the voters in Massachusetts.

While Richard Nixon was hated by most of the major media, whose "star" anchormen, reporters and editors attacked him with vitriolic vigor, his record as President was just too good to ignore. The majority of the electorate were middle Americans, to whom the President related personally, and who benefited most from his accomplishments in office. They had lived through the Johnson administration and were not going to swallow the line that Vietnam was "Nixon's War".

The American presence in Vietnam had been reduced from over 500,000 in 1968 to 69,000 in 1972. Judicious use of American power in Cambodia and Laos had forestalled North Vietnamese invasions in 1970 and in 1971, and it looked as though Vietnamization was going to succeed. The President's tough reaction to the 1972 spring invasion had all but stopped the war. There wasn't much for McGovern to hang his campaign hat on, and his avowed radical policies put off many traditional Democratic backers. The Vietnam War had been McGovern's main issue, and America's role in it was clearly diminishing. George McGovern conceded the election before election day 1972 was over. Richard Nixon had won reelection by a landslide, piling up the largest popular vote total in the history of presidential politics.

F-4E of 366th TFW taxies past an HH-53C Super Jolly Green Giant at Danang AB. (USAF)

HH-53C of the 37th ARRS, which was based at Danang throughout the war. It is at Phu Cat on 7 July, 1971, where it had been temporarily deployed to avoid a typhoon. (Norman E. Taylor)

40th ARRS HH-53 escorted by a pair of 1st SOS A-1s on a September, 1972, rescue mission into North Vietnam. (USAF)

(Below) 40th ARRS HH-53C over the jungles of Laos. Miniguns were mounted on the rear ramp, and in the right and left forward crew doors. (USAF)

(Above) The primary defensive armament of the HH-53 rescue helicopter was the minigun, which was capable of cyclic rates of fire of 4,000 rounds per minute. (USAF)

(Below) The rescue of downed aircrew deep in enemy territory was made possible by aerial refuelling of helicopters, a concept that was developed and proven during the Vietnam War. Here an HC-130P refuels an HH-53C on 23 May, 1972. (USAF)

With the resumed intensity of the air war over North Vietnam during May of 1972, members of the Command and Control team had to use mobile control facilities to keep the flight line at Takhli running until permanent systems could be reactivated. (USAF)

The C-9A Nightingale is the military version of the McDonnell Douglas DC-9. Seen here evacuating patients from Ubon AB, Thailand, to Clark AFB, Philippines. (USAF)

A-7s and F-4s refuel from a KC-135 during LINEBACKER II mission in December, 1972. (USAF)

RF-4C of the 432nd TRS. The name on the centerline tank reads "BARREL SHARKS", possibly an allusion to "Barrel Roll", which was the code name for Laos.

(Above) An RF-4C photographed this squadron of F-4s headed for North Vietnam. Obviously the photograph was shot in a no-threat area, since the formation is definitely non-tactical! (USAF via Captain Wally Van Winkle)

(Below) RF-4C, 65-0849 of the 11th TRS, 432nd TRW, was named "El Bandido", and carried an elaborate cartoon on the splitter plate. (USAF via Captain Wally Van Winkle)

The gigantic C-5A was a key factor in the quick buildup of aerial forces required for LINEBACKER operations. Seen here taking off from Udorn AB on 4 January, 1972. (USAF)

Offloading the equipment necessary to reopen Takhli during May of 1972. (USAF)

(Above) A-7D of the 354th TFW during a rescue escort mission. In addition to its computer-aided bombing accuracy, the A-7 proved itself in the "Sandy" role. (LTV)

(Below) Aircrew quarters at Takhli were not luxurious, but they were air conditioned and comfortable. Base transportation is parked at the front door. (B/G Don Kutyna)

F-4D of the 8th TFW loaded with a pair of KMU-390 electro-optically guided bombs, another branch of the "Smart Bomb" family. This Phantom II is also equipped with an ECM pod on the left forward Sparrow Missile well as it taxies for a May, 1972, mission against North Vietnam. (USAF)

F-4D of the 432nd TRW prepares for an October, 1972, mission from Udorn. (USAF)

F-4D of the 49th TFW at Takhli RTAB taxies past "Rocket Alley Alice". (John Santucci)

GIA LAM RR YARD & SHOPS

18 PIECES ROLLING STOCK DAMAGED/DESTROYED

CRANEWAY DAMAGED

6 SUPPORT BUILDINGS DESTROYED

16 DAMAGED BUILDINGS

→ DAMAGED BUILDING
↩ DESTROYED BUILDING
◯ TRACK INTERDICTION

The Gia Lam Railroad yard and shops were one of the primary targets of LINEBACKER II operations. Post Strike photo shows the effectiveness of the B-52 bombing. (USAF)

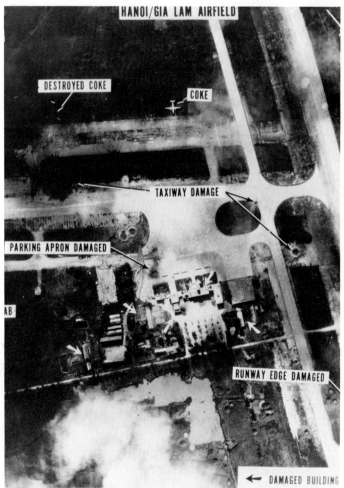

HANOI/GIA LAM AIRFIELD

DESTROYED COKE   COKE

TAXIWAY DAMAGE

PARKING APRON DAMAGED

AB

RUNWAY EDGE DAMAGED

← DAMAGED BUILDING

Hanoi/Gia Lam airport was struck for the first time in the war during LINEBACKER II. This 21 December, 1972, photo shows damage of previous day's strike. (USAF)

A pair of laser bombers of the 8th TFW, in formation with the laser designator equipped F-4 during a September, 1972, strike against North Vietnam. (USAF)

F-4D of the 497th TFS, 8th TFW, in the wash rack at Ubon RTAB.

A-1E of VNAF 23rd Tactical Wing during a 1971 close air support mission.

F-4D of the 13th TFS, 432nd TRW, opened up for maintenance at Udorn RTAB during the Christmas stand-down of LINEBACKER II, December, 1972. (Harley Copic)

(Above Right) F-4E being prepped for a mission to Route Pak Six (Hanoi/Haiphong) during LINEBACKER II. The Phantom II is TDY from the 4th TFS to the 555th TFS, 432nd TRW, Udorn RTAB. (Harley Copic)

RF-4C of the 14th TRS at Udorn RTAB, summer, 1973. (Ron Thurlow)

During the buildup of forces in Southeast Asia for LINEBACKER I operations, aircraft were drawn from several stateside units, and carried the markings of their former units into combat. A former 4th TFW F-4E lands at Ubon, the base of the 8th TFW. (USAF)

Steve Ritchie became the first USAF ace (and the only pilot-ace) of the war on 28 August, 1972, when he shot down his fifth MiG with a Sparrow AAM. All of Ritchie's kills were with the AIM-7 Sparrow, and all were MiG-21s. He flew with the 555th TFS, 432nd TRW, out of Udorn RTAB. (USAF)

F-4D of the 8th TFW and F-4E of the 388th TFW refuel at dawn inbound to targets in North Vietnam. (Don Logan)

F-105G of Detachment 1, 561st TFS, Korat RTAB, carried the inscription "CAN'T MACK IT TO IT" on the intake. Seen here enroute to North Vietnam on a SAM suppression mission. It carries Shrike ARM missiles. (USAF)

Armament specialist checking the mounting lugs on 500-lb. bombs aboard a B-52D prior to an ARC LIGHT strike against tactical targets in South Vietnam. (USAF)

LINEBACKER II

On December 17, the Joint Chiefs of Staff sent the following message to CINCPAC, CINCSAC, and operational commanders within Seventh Air Force:

YOU ARE DIRECTED TO COMMENCE AT APPROXIMATELY 1200Z, 18 DECEMBER, 1972, A THREE-DAY MAXIMUM EFFORT, REPEAT, MAXIMUM EFFORT, OF B-52/TACAIR STRIKES IN THE HANOI/HAIPHONG AREAS AGAINST THE TARGETS CONTAINED IN THE AUTHORIZED TARGET LIST. OBJECT IS MAXIMUM DESTRUCTION OF SELECTED MILITARY TARGETS IN THE VICINITY OF HANOI/HAIPHONG. BE PREPARED TO EXTEND OPERATIONS PAST THREE DAYS, IF DIRECTED.

FOLLOWING INSTRUCTIONS APPLY:

A. UTILIZE VISUAL AS WELL AS ALL-WEATHER CAPABILITIES.

B. UTILIZE ALL RESOURCES WHICH CAN BE SPARED WITHOUT CRITICAL DETRIMENT TO OPERATIONS IN RVN AND SUPPORT OF EMERGENCY SITUATIONS IN LAOS AND CAMBODIA.

C. UTILIZE RESTRIKES ON AUTHORIZED TARGETS AS NECESSARY. NORTH VIETNAMESE AIR ORDER OF BATTLE, AIRFIELDS, AND ACTIVE SURFACE-TO-AIR MISSILE SITES MAY BE STRUCK AS TACTICAL SITUATION DICTATES TO IMPROVE EFFECTIVENESS OF ATTACK FORCES AND MINIMIZE LOSSES.

D. EXERCISE PRECAUTION TO MINIMIZE RISK OF CIVILIAN CASUALTIES UTILIZING LGB WEAPONS AGAINST DESIGNATED TARGETS. AVOID DAMAGE TO THIRD-COUNTRY SHIPPING.

CW-2 Neal Thompson caught an NVA PT-76 out in the open in the Que Son Valley, south of Danang, in 1972. Though the 2.75 rockets could not penetrate the tank's armor, the repeated hammering on its hull killed the crew and disabled the tank.

CH-53 of HM-12 sweeping Haiphong Harbor for mines which were laid at the beginning of LINEBACKER I. (US Navy)

(Left) CH-53 of HMH-463 operating off USS Tripoli in Haiphong Harbor during OPERATION END SWEEP in 1973.

F-4B of VF-161, which got five MiGs during LINEBACKER operations, including the last Navy MiG Kill of the war on 12 January, 1973. (Duane Kasulka via Charles Howes)

Lou Drendel
1983

F-4D of the 13th TFS, 432nd TRW, as it appeared during the summer of 1973, while operating from Udorn RTAB.

A pair of F-4Js of VF-143 on the initial go-around before landing on USS Enterprise in the South China Sea, 31 August, 1971. (US Navy)

The planners, both civilian and military, knew that the greatly increased aerial defenses around Hanoi and Haiphong would make these missions dangerous. But the President was convinced of their necessity, and he put the onus on the military by telling Admiral Moorer, Chairman of JCS, "This is your chance to use military power effectively to win this war, and if you don't, I'll consider you responsible."

Six B-52s were shot down by SAMs on 20 December. This caused a reduction in the number of B-52 sorties while ECM tactics were refined to provide better defenses against SAMs, and reconnaissance aircraft searched for SAM storage and assembly areas. One of the major SAM assembly areas was located in a heavily populated area of Hanoi. Poor weather precluded the use of smart bombs on this target, and its size ruled out the use of B-52s. One of the most notable missions of the war was the destruction of this target by 16 LORAN guided F-4s, which bombed from 20,000 feet through solid overcast. 48 SAMS were fired at the formation, which remained rock-steady throughout the bomb run. None of the F-4s were lost, and civilian casualties were minimal. This raid helped to take some of the heat off the B-52s, which had run a gauntlet of 220 SAMs on December 20.

The B-52 raids had lost a total of 11 airplanes in the first three days of LINEBACKER II, and the crews blamed many of those losses on tactics. The BUFs were just too big and too heavy afoot to use the same SAM-evading tactics employed by fighters. Their only salvation was concentrated jamming of the SAM guidance radars. This was accomplished by flying precise formations of three aircraft cells. Each aircraft in the formation contributed its jamming capability to the integrity of the formation. If one aircraft dropped out of the formation, not only was he making himself vulnerable to SAMs, he was also decreasing the chances of the other two aircraft avoiding SAMs. Additionally, steep turns away from the target had the effect of "tilting" the jamming beams away from potential attackers, making the bombers more vulnerable. Revised tactics prevented any further B-52 losses prior to the Christmas stand-down. The President ordered all missions cancelled for 24 hours on Christmas Day, but in spite of pressure from his staff to continue the bombing halt, he ordered the biggest, and what was to be the most effective, B-52 raid of the war on the 26th.

Using new tactics, which called for tightly packed bomber streams striking their targets within the space of fifteen minutes, from various altitudes, and from different directions, one hundred-sixteen B-52s devastated targets in Hanoi and Haiphong. They were supported by a variety of tactical aircraft, including F-105 and A-7E Iron Hand SAM killers, F-4 Chaff Bombers, F-4 MIGCAP fighters, and EB-66, EA-3A, EA-6 ECM support aircraft from USAF, USN, and USMC squadrons. The total of over 100 support aircraft also included strikes on selected MiG bases and SAM sites by all-weather F-111s and A-6s. Ten targets were struck by the B-52s, for the loss of two aircraft (one over Hanoi, and one which crashed short of the Utapao runway as a result of battle damage). It was probably this mission, more than any other, that demonstrated to the North Vietnamese that Richard Nixon was not going to allow them to continue the war on their terms. Several POWs reported that their captors underwent drastic personality modification as a result of this mission and those that followed. In a word, they were scared cross-eyed!

On the 27th sixty B-52s returned to Hanoi. The thirty aircraft from Guam and thirty from Utapao attacked SAM sites as well as strategic targets. Two more aircraft were lost, one to a SAM site it had just attacked. During this mission and some of the previous missions, MiGs had flown loose formation with some of the B-52 cells. Intelligence surmised that the MiGs were pacing the BUFs for SAMs and AAA. No B-52s were lost to MiGs, but B-52 tail gunners were credited with shooting down two MiGs during LINEBACKER II. More SAMS were fired at the B-52s on the 27th than on any previous mission, but with poorer accuracy. Some crews thought that the North Vietnamese were firing in salvoes, hoping for a lucky hit. The enemy effort on the night of the 27th smacked of desperation. It was the last strong attempt at defending their capital, and when it failed, there was not much doubt about the outcome of the war.

The B-52s returned to North Vietnam twice more before the communists caved in, agreeing to return to the Paris talks on 2 January. On 29 December all bombing above the 20th parallel was halted. The North Vietnamese propaganda mill churned out charges of "extermination bombing", and the liberal media echoed these charges with their own accusations of "carpet bombing". By their own accounting, the North Vietnamese lost between 1,300 and 1,400 civilians during LINEBACKER II. Many of these casualties were caused by SAM missiles that went ballistic and exploded in populated areas. But even had all the casualties been caused by B-52s, it would have been the lowest loss ratio per bomb tonnage in the history of aerial warfare. (.08 deaths per ton of bombs, contrasted with 1.06 in the bombing of Coventry on 14 November, 1940, or the appalling figure of 50.33 in the fire bombing of Tokyo on 9-10 March, 1945.) Many in the media compared LINEBACKER II to the bombing campaigns of World War II in terms of collateral civilian damage. It was another case of the press not allowing facts to interfere with their version of history.

Checking M-117 750-lb. GP bombs prior to loading on a B-52D at Andersen AFB, Guam, during LINEBACKER II. (USAF)

Fusing Mk.82 500-lb. bombs aboard a B-52D. (USAF)

B-52 loading operations during LINEBACKER II. (USAF)

LINEBACKER II was a maximum effort operation, which meant doing whatever was necessary to get the B-52s in the air. This D model is getting an engine change after bombs were loaded. (USAF)

(Above) B-52D being prepared for a LINEBACKER II mission. (USAF)

The lack of wing droop and empty pylons indicates that this BUF is returning from a mission. It is probably a quarter of a million pounds lighter than it was at takeoff! (USAF)

F-8 Crusader being pulled to a halt. Deck crewman is letting the pilot know that he has caught the arresting gear and can pull the power off.

HH-43F "Pedro" at Bien Hoa, 1971. The Kamman HH-43 was used for airbase rescue and crash fire fighting. (Wayne Mutza)

(Right) SP-5 Ramiro Ramirez (on the left) and WO-1 Joseph M. Long of the 240th AHC loading 2.75 rockets on a UH-1M of the 240th gun platoon "Mad Dogs" at Camp Bear Cat, January, 1971. (US Army via Wayne Mutza)

UH-1H of the 162nd AHC on LZ 48, Danang, summer of 1971. (Mike Campbell)

One of the diverse aircraft pressed into ICCS service was this civil-registered (N91572) Volpar conversion of the twin Beech. (US Army)

Loading a B-52 for LINEBACKER II strikes on Hanoi, December, 1972. (USAF)

A-4F of VA-164 about to launch from USS Hancock for a 1971 combat mission. "Lady Jessie" was flown by Cdr. Fred Gosebrikk.

BUF (Big Ugly Fellow) enroute to the target. B-52s carried 500 and 750-lb. bombs in loads of up to 60,000 lbs. (USAF)

B-52 returning after a mission. The primary base for the big bombers throughout the war was Andersen AFB, Guam. With the advent of LINEBACKER operations, B-52s were based at Utapao AB in Thailand, which greatly shortened mission times, allowing more frequent scheduling of crews. (USAF)

B-52 has just flared for landing. The unique tandem landing gear has been adjusted for crosswind crab so that the aircraft fuselage will be on runway heading on landing. (USAF)

Approach angle is relatively flat in the B-52. (USAF)

Maintenance continued throughout tropical rains which produced this reflecting pool on a taxiway. (USAF)

B-52s made a moonscape of the Ai Mo warehouse complex during Linebacker. (USAF)

The Hanoi Fabrication Plant was gutted by a B-52 strike. (USAF)

A portion of the Kinh No rail yard. Twenty-four of thirty bulldozers were damaged by B-52 strikes when they were caught in the yard. Two large warehouses were destroyed in the same raid. (USAF)

Phuc Yen, one of North Vietnam's principal MiG bases, was put out of business by B-52 interdiction strikes which cut runways and tax-iways. (USAF)

Some of the men who went to Hanoi in B-52s react to results of one of their missions in a briefing. (USAF)

USAF HH-53 Super Jolly Green Giant was the premier rescue helicopter throughout the last years of the US involvement. Seen here over the fogshrouded mountains of Laos, enroute to North Vietnam.

VNAF CH-34 carried no markings on its unusual two-tone green camouflage. Bien Hoa, 1971. (Wayne Mutza)

VNAF A-37 out of Binh Thuy. (Pham Quang Kheim)

One of two TOW Missile equipped UH-1Bs sent to Vietnam after the Easter invasion. The two Hueys, flown by six different pilots, scored 73 hits out of the first 89 missiles fired in the first combat use of the TOW missile system. (Bell Helicopter)

On 23 May, 1972, LCDR Mugs McKeown and Lt. Jack Ensch got in a fight with MiG-19s and MiG-17s. The MiG-19s got away, two of the MiG-17s did not.

VNAF UH-1H armed with XM-21 and XM-175 systems during August of 1971. (USAF via Wayne Mutza)

1973: PEACE AND PULLOUT

When Henry Kissinger returned to the Paris talks, he found that the North Vietnamese were no longer stalling. They had made up their minds that Richard Nixon would not be swayed by either congressional or public pressures, and that the implied threat to continue the bombing of Hanoi could not be discounted. This in spite of the fact that the Democratic Congress had voted to cut off funds for military operations in Vietnam as soon as American POWs were released. The Democrats in Congress had removed any doubt about their collective attitude concerning the partisanship of the issue of how the United States got out of Vietnam. When it became obvious that Nixon and Kissinger were going to end the war on the United States' terms, the Democratic leadership tried to cash in on this success by claiming they had acted in a ''responsible and non-partisan'' manner during the latest talks. On 11 January the North Vietnamese agreed to the entire text of the agreement. The only obstacle to peace now was President Thieu of South Vietnam.

Once again it was Alexander Haig who drew the assignment of telling Thieu that President Nixon was committed to signing the agreement, with or without Theiu's blessing. While the Vietnamese, North and South, may have been fooled by Nixon's tough stance in the negotiations, Nixon himself realized that the political fact of the matter was that the United States would no longer support the war. One way or another, the US was ''bugging out''. Though Thieu was unhappy with the agreement, he had only two options. If he failed to go along, the US Congress would certainly cut off aid immediately. If, on the other hand, he went along with the peace agreement, he would continue to receive economic and military aid from the United States. Most importantly, he had Nixon's promise that the United States would ''react strongly in the event the agreement is violated.'' He was finally pressured into going along with the agreement, though not without several bitter exchanges. None of the other members of SEATO had any illusions about the honor of the North Vietnamese. They knew, as Thieu knew, that the communists would continue to attack South Vietnam to the extent possible without bringing retaliation. Nguyen Cao Ky, in an interview with the CIA's General Charles Timmes, in March, 1973, warned that the communists would not honor the agreements. He said, ''They will not respect them because they have got the Americans out and that is the biggest victory the communists have ever had. But it is not the first. They chased out the French and now, in a sense, they have chased out the Americans. I give them a couple of years before they invade the South.''

South Vietnamese leaders were particularly bitter because they knew how badly beaten the North was at that moment. Its industry had ceased to exist, and its people were on the verge of starvation. North Vietnam existed at the forebearance of the Soviet Union. Thieu and Ky felt that better terms and more insurance for a lasting peace could have been achieved if the United States had been willing to tough it out a little longer. This view was obviously not shared by the American leaders, who were anxious to have the war behind them so that they could concentrate on other aspects of foreign and domestic policy.

Under the terms of the agreement, signed on 27 January, 1973, the United States would withdraw the 60,000 troops remaining in South Vietnam. The North Vietnamese would return all POWS. In President Nixon's words, it was ''Peace with Honor''. America had spent over 56,000 lives and 130 billion dollars to defend a country of 17 million people half-way around the world. In terms of honoring treaty commitments, it was indeed peace with honor. As far as a majority of Americans was concerned, we had done our duty and it was time to get out. If the South Vietnamese were worthy, they would survive. Most people were not willing to assess our involvement in terms of how wisely we spent lives or money. The fact that we spent so much meant that we had done all we could have been expected to have done, regardless of the ultimate outcome.

The national euphoria experienced during OPERATION HOMECOMING, the return of the POWs, was hardly akin to the VE and VJ day celebrations of World War II. But the war was over, and the emerging fact that the North Vietnamese were a nation of barbarians, whose only growth industry was war, who never honored a commitment unless forced to do so, whose treatment of prisoners indicated that perhaps they should have been ''bombed back into the Stone Age'', and who were quite obviously going to continue the war, did not change the public's relief that the United States was out of Vietnam.

America was out of Vietnam, but not out of Southeast Asia. US Military headquarters was shifted from Saigon to Nakhon Phanom Air Base in Thailand, while the US embassy in Saigon maintained a largely civilian military attache's office. Opponents of the war in the United States continued to press for a complete withdrawal of military aid to the South, claiming that the South Vietnamese government was corrupt and unworthy of American support. In point of fact, the government in the south was as close to being completely democratic as you might have reasonably expected any nation to be, faced as it was with extinction. The antiwar forces hypocritically did not apply their high moral standards to the North Vietnamese or their Russian sponsors. The antiwar movement in the United States had become an anti-American movement, doing its best to subvert the government and polarize the population.

8th TFW F-4D prepares for a June, 1973, mission from Ubon RTAB. (USAF)

F-4E of the 8th TFW returning to Ubon after a 1973 bombing mission over Cambodia. This aircraft was transferred from Eglin AFB during the spring of 1972, and still carried the tail codes of the 33rd TFW a year later. (USAF)

432nd TRW Headquarters at Udorn. As the principal MIGCAP unit, the 432nd produced the only USAF aces of the war. They displayed their scoreboard over the front door. (Ron Thurlow)

They found fertile ground for their seeds of discontent in Washington. The Democrats controlled Congress, the media, the bureaucracy, and the power brokers who operated behind the scenes. The Republicans had only the White House. The Presidency would come under increasing siege from these disparate forces during 1973 and 1974, and Richard Nixon would eventually be forced to resign as a result of that "two-bit burglary" at the Watergate. The hue and cry that accompanied the on-going media event could not have been more effectively orchestrated for the benefit of the communists had it been scripted in Hanoi. While Richard Nixon was President, there was still the threat of retaliation if the communists broke the peace agreements. When he was gone, the Democratic Congress would be able to completely cut aid to South Vietnam.

F-4D loaded with 2,000-lb. laser-guided bombs at Udorn, summer of 1973. The formerly "permissive" environment of Cambodia had been so packed with AAA by 1973 that strike aircraft were required to carry their own ECM protection. (Ron Thurlow)

F-4D, 66-249, on a Sky Spot radar bombing mission over Cambodia in the summer of 1973. Known as "SKY PUKE", 249 was the first D model to shoot down a MiG. (Ron Thurlow)

(Below) Steve Ritchie's 463 leaving Udorn for Ubon, where it would complete the war assigned to the 8th TFW. (Ron Thurlow)

RF-4C taxies at Korat during the summer of 1973. It carries two ECM pods. (Bob Baldo)

RF-8G of VFP-63 about to get the launch signal. As "The Eyes of the Fleet", VFP-63 operated detachments aboard several attack carriers throughout the war.

(Left) Maintaining a 23rd Tactical Wing A-1 at Bien Hoa, 1971. (Wayne Mutza)

(Below Left) A-1 fresh from the overhaul facility at Bien Hoa, December, 1971. (Wayne Mutza)

(Below) VNAF A-37 at Bien Hoa, December, 1971. (Wayne Mutza)

F-4s take on fuel enroute to targets in Cambodia during the summer of 1973. (Ron Thurlow)

(Left) F-105G Wild Weasels of the 17th Wild Weasel Squadron at Korat in 1973. (Bob Baldo)

F-4E of the 388th TFW at Korat in 1974. (Bob Baldo)

HC-130P on the ramp at Korat. In addition to its rescue and refueling duties, this version of the Herk was used for command and control duties. (Bob Baldo)

(Below) F-111As were still flying missions over Southeast Asia in 1973. The F-111 was one of the most effective interdiction aircraft during linebacker operations, flying solo low and fast, using terrain-following radar to stay under NVA radars. (Ron Thurlow)

OV-10A of the 23rd Tactical Air Support Squadron backing into its parking spot after the unit's last mission was flown, 15 August, 1973. (USAF)

Unusual choppers are displayed on an A-7D of the 354th TFW. (Bob Baldo)

OPERATION HOMECOMING

Almost from the beginning of hostilities, there was national concern of varying degrees over the plight of the POWs. Though North Vietnam was a signatory of the 1949 Geneva Convention on the treatment of Prisoners of War, they quickly disclaimed any responsibility for observing these rules, claiming that no formal declaration of war existed. (The Geneva Convention did not acknowledge this semantic.) The communists threatened to treat POWs as war criminals, staging trials and executions. However, reaction to this threat was so overwhelmingly negative that the communists quickly dropped it. Had they in fact followed through with their threats, some of their most ardent supporters in the United States would have been silenced in the storm of public outrage that would have demanded heavy retribution. Senator Richard Russell warned that North Vietnam would be turned into a desert, and Senator George Aiken said that North Vietnam would be completely destroyed if any executions of POWs took place.

While they dropped their public threats against the POWs, the North Vietnamese continued to mistreat their prisoners. The PQWs were subjected to incredible physical and psychological torture. Though the South Vietnamese opened their prison camps to the International Red Cross, and allowed their prisoners mail privileges, the North Vietnamese would allow neither of these to American POWs (because of the treatment of American POWs, the communists were forced to hide them, since any objective observer would have realized immediately that the communists were torturing helpless prisoners).

Eventually the communists did allow visits by decidedly nonobjective observers. Members of US antiwar groups were allowed to visit Hanoi, and some of the prisoners. These were pure propaganda ploys, which the North Vietnamese overplayed by releasing nine of the POWs in three groups of three, each to a different antiwar faction. The first two groups were released during the Johnson Administration. The third was released in July, 1969. Though warned by the North Vietnamese not to "embarrass" them, these POWs spoke out during a news conference held in September. Lt. Robert F. Frishman and Seaman Douglas Hegdahl revealed the torture, beatings, lack of proper medical treatment, and solitary confinement routinely dished out by the communists. This publicity caused a strong negative reaction to the communists, allowing President Nixon to pursue a harder line in the war. It also brought the families of the POWs together in a manner never before possible. Their cause received more publicity, and an outpouring of sympathy from the American people. This cause did not die with the return of 591 American POWs in 1973. The plight of over 2500 MIAs remains a virtual mystery, and ten years after the end of the war, there is still pressure for a satisfactory resolution of the fate of these men.

The POWs had become a very visible issue during the war, and the Administration worked at keeping this issue in the court of world opinion. In 1970 President Nixon appointed Astronaut Colonel Frank Borman as Special Representative on Prisoners of War, and Borman's trip to 14 countries, including the Soviet Union, kept the pressure on North Vietnam. The National League of Families held their first convention that year. All of this publicity had the effect of guaranteeing that there would be no settlement of the war...no peace...without the return of the POWs.

When the peace agreements were finally negotiated, the only thing the United States actually got was the release of the POWs. This had become the be-all, end-all of the war for most Americans, and with the announcement that the POWs were coming home, "peace with honor" became a buzz phrase for satisfactory terms for getting out of Vietnam. The return of the POWs was dubbed OPERATION HOMECOMING, and it had been in the planning stages for several years when the peace agreements were finally signed in January of 1973. These agreements called for phased release of the POWs, coinciding with withdrawal of American troops.

When the repatriation of prisoners finally came, it was the brightest moment in all the long years of war. There were innumerable incidents that verified the indomitable spirit of these most courageous of American fighting men. In spite of the low-key welcome and readjustment period planned by the Pentagon, the national euphoria that accompanied the homecoming resulted in an outpouring of spontaneous emotion. As President Nixon told Frank Fitzsimmons, head of the Teamsters, "I was never prouder to be an American". The war that was too unpopular to produce heroes had finally produced heroes that all Americans were proud of. "Peace with Honor" did mean return of prisoners who honored their country by performing heroically. "Peace with Honor" did not mean reacting to the horrors imposed upon those men during their years of captivity in the manner in which an America of an earlier age might have.

When all of the POWs had been returned, the story of their imprisonment emerged in all its grisly detail. Torture, physical and psychological, was practiced on a regular basis by the North Vietnamese. At least 55 of the prisoners who had died in captivity were believed to have succumbed as a result of torture. The Senators and Congressmen who promised that North Vietnam would be turned into a desert if any prisoners were executed were mute when proof of executions was made public by returning POWs. The nation took pride in the saga of the "4th Combined POW Wing". They shared in the joyous homecoming emotions. They did not thirst after vengeance for the barbaric treatment of their countrymen.

A-7Ds of the 3rd TFS, 388th TFW, took part in the rescue of the Mayaguez in April, 1975. They were based at Korat RTAB. (LTV)

Boeing CH-47C Chinook at Phu Cat during July, 1971. The "Hook", more often called "shithook", was the primary medium-lift helicopter of the war. (Norman E. Taylor)

CH-47 of the 1st Cavalry at Camp Bear Cat in 1971. The cargo lift hook bay is open. (Wayne Mutza)

This Chinook was transferred from the US Army to the Australians. Bear Cat 1971. (Wayne Mutza)

(Below Left) 1st Air Cav CH-47, 362nd Lift Company, with its cargo ramp down at Bear Cat. (Wayne Mutza)

"Blow Your Mind" was also assigned to the 362nd Lift Company at Bear Cat in 1971. (Wayne Mutza)

"RAGGEDY ANN" was assigned to the 132nd Assault Helicopter Company, 14th Combat Aviation Battalion at Chu Lai, 1971. (Mike Campbell)

During a maintenance runup, this Chinook of the 362nd got away, jumped vertically out of its revetment, spun around twice, and rolled over, "beating itself to death". Though pieces of rotor blades were thrown up to 300 yards, piercing hangar walls, no one was hurt. (Ralph Hood)

No Comment. (Wayne Mutza)

"WAR WAGON" was assigned to the 362nd at Bear Cat during 1971. (Wayne Mutza)

CH-47C of the 1st Cav. The C model was equipped with uprated twin 3,750 hp T-55L-11A engines, which allowed it to lift 30,000 lbs. of external load. (Wayne Mutza)

Chinook unloads supplies on a hilltop outpost in the highlands. (US Army)

(Left) A freak accident destroyed this Phu Cat based C-7. It was on short final for landing at Ha Thanh when it was struck by an outgoing round from a US artillery battery on the perimeter of the camp. A cease-fire order had been issued, but was not received by the battery commander. (via Ron Verner)

(Below Left) Beech U-21A was used as a light cargo transport by the Army before being reassigned to Air America, the CIA airline in Southeast Asia. (F. C. Brown)

(Below) DeHavilland U-6A Beaver was flown in support of intelligence collection missions in western Pleiku and Kontum Provinces. By the fall of 1973, when this photo was taken, inactivity at Camp Holloway in Pleiku had encouraged the grass in its takeover of the parking revetments. (Andy L. Mutzig)

1973-74—BEGINNINGS OF THE END

While all of America was celebrating the return of the POWs and the "end" of the war, the North Vietnamese were busily preparing for yet another attack on the South. Even before the last US combat troops were withdrawn from South Vietnam, the communists had moved 30,000 troops and 300 tracked vehicles, including 200 tanks, into staging areas in Laos, Cambodia, and South Vietnam. SA-2 SAM missile sites were observed ringing the former US Marine combat base at Khe Sanh, where the North Vietnamese had repaired the airstrip and inserted their own garrison of troops in clear violation of the peace agreements. The missile sites "disappeared" as a result of US State Department protests, but were believed to have only been moved to camouflaged positions nearby. The ink was not even dry on the peace agreements which called for removal of all foreign troops from Laos, and the North Vietnamese were already testing Nixon's admonition that violations of the agreement would result in "strong reaction" by the United States. When that strong reaction failed to materialize (President Nixon was increasingly occupied with domestic problems related to Watergate), it became obvious that the South would have to fend for itself.

The ultimate goal of Vietnamization had always been for South Vietnam to be able to defend itself, and several programs were instituted to obtain this goal. Projects ENHANCE and ENHANCE PLUS were launched in late 1972 in an effort to replace combat material lost in the 1972 offensive, and to further strengthen all branches of the South Vietnamese armed forces, which were expected to have 1.1 million men under arms in 1973. These programs provided the following additional aircraft to VNAF: 286 UH-1, 23 CH-47, 22 AC-119K, 28 A-1, 32 C-130, 90 A-37, 4 C-7, 118 F-5A & B, 23 EC-47, 24 T-37, and 35 O-2, which were exchanged on a one-for-one basis with O-1s. These shipments began arriving at Tan Son Nhut in October of 1972, and lasted throughout December. In addition to the aircraft, large stocks of ammunition, artillery, vehicles of all types, and other supplies were in place at the culmination of these programs.

Cessna O-1G of the 219th R A Company at Phu Cat AB, 27 February, 1971. (Norman E. Taylor)

While the United States was withdrawing its military presence from South Vietnam, it did make plans for the defense of South Vietnam through the application of airpower. The organization responsible for implementing such a plan was the United States Support Activities Group/Seventh Air Force, based at Nakhon Phanom Air Base in Thailand. From this base the USSAG/7th AF directed air operations in Cambodia until August of 1973, when Congress cut off funds for the continuation of military assistance. The communists had never abided by the terms of the cease-fire agreements in Cambodia, and it was only the use of American air power that prevented a North Vietnamese victory in Cambodia sooner. It is to the credit of the Cambodian government that they were able to resist the attacks of Khymer Rouge, NVA, and VC troops for as long as they did.

In the meantime, the communists continued to strengthen their position in the south, bringing additional 37mm and 57mm AAA and SAM missiles into defensive positions around airfields from the DMZ to Thien Ngon, just north of Saigon. The VNAF, lacking the sophisticated electronic countermeasures equipment to attack these positions, were powerless to stop this build-up. By the end of 1974 the air defenses of North Vietnam, imported to the South, had reduced the effectiveness of tactical airlift, and had made the helicopter virtually useless in air assaults or resupply of forward combat positions. The VNAF had placed 224 aircraft in flyable storage, including all of its A-1s which were considered near the end of their operational lives anyway. They had lost 299 aircraft in combat or accidents.

The super powers had turned Vietnam into a war of attrition, and in a war of attrition, as in a high stakes poker game, staying power determines the ultimate winner. The Soviets were unstinting in their support of the North Vietnamese, while the US Congress was increasingly reluctant when it came to military aid for the South Vietnamese. The South Vietnamese armed forces had been made over in the image of the American military, where vast amounts of ammunition were often expended on minimal targets. Granted, this practice had grown out of the frustration that resulted from political constraints which prevented more effective, and possibly prudent, application of military power. But the net effect of these policies was to up the ante, and the Russians matched the Americans at each step along the way. In 1973 the Viet-

namese, North and South, had two of the largest armies in the world. Both had effective leadership and good equipment. But it was the North which was on the attack. The South simply did not have the wherewithal to attack North Vietnam. They were forced to fight a series of holding actions, while the North continued to pour men and materiel into the South. During most of 1973 there was little fighting, as the communists concentrated on improving their logistical systems and consolidating their positions in the roughly twenty-five percent of South Vietnam that they controlled at the time of the cease-fire.

Considering the demonstrated American largess in providing other nations with sophisticated aircraft, the question may well be asked why the VNAF was never provided with anything hotter than F-5s. There was no question that their VNAF could not operate their aircraft in the air defense environment created by the highly effective Soviet anti-aircraft weaponry being imported into the South by the NVA. The answer may lie in the aggressiveness of some of South Vietnam's leaders. Nguyen Cao Ky, while he was head of the VNAF, begged for the opportunity to strike at the enemy homeland. Had he been given the equipment to fly regular bombing missions into the North, it is doubtful that he would have observed the same rules of engagement imposed on US pilots by Washington. The VNAF could be held in check by limiting what it was given to use against the enemy. While the US was still in the war the VNAF was relegated to interdiction and close support missions against targets in the South. When the US withdrew, the VNAF was left to face the world's toughest air combat environment with aircraft that were clearly not up to the task. Their principal combat aircraft were the A-1, A-37, and F-5A/B. The A-1 was a World War II vintage piston-engined dive bomber. The A-37 was a trainer-turned-bomber meant to be employed in the relatively permissive environment envisioned in the Counterinsurgency (COIN) mission. The F-5 had no fire control radar. So, while the US left the VNAF with a force of over 2,000 aircraft, there was widespread doubt within knowledgeable circles that the VNAF would be able to maintain this force, or employ it effectively against the NVA air defenses. The tremendous expan-

The layers of dust were redistributed every time the huge CH-54 Flying Crane delivered supplies to fire bases. (Ron Botz)

"TRAVELER", a UH-1H of the 11th Armored Cavalry Regiment. (Glenn Horton)

The addition of miniguns to Army Hueys gave them devastating firepower. (Ron Burns)

Action at LZ Snoopy, 1971. Hueys are from the 116th Assault Helicopter Company. (Mike Campbell)

Hueys at Camp Evans in 1971. (Ron Lauer)

sion of the VNAF was reason enough for these pessimistic prognostications: from less than 400 aircraft in 1968 to over 2,000 in late 1972; from seventeen squadrons in 1968 to sixty squadrons in 1972, and from 17,000 personnel in 1968 to 65,000 in 1972. The traditional reluctance of the VNAF to fly in bad weather or at night caused further problems.

The United States Congress passed the Cooper-Church Amendment in August of 1973, restraining the President's authority to commit forces to Laos, Cambodia, or Vietnam. It was a clear signal to the North Vietnamese, the United States would not act upon any further aggression. The only American aid to the South would come in the form of military equipment, and the United States had already demonstrated that it did not intend to provide the South with an offensive capability. The communists reacted to this piece of good news by further stripping their air defenses in the North, sending them south. Virtually the entire North Vietnamese army was free to invade South Vietnam. Though President Nixon admonished Congress not to tie his hands, saying, "After more than ten arduous years of suffering and sacrifice...it would be nothing short of tragic if this great accomplishment, bought with the blood of so many Asians and Americans, were to be undone now by Congressional action". They did just that. The effect of this was immediately apparent in negotiations with the Russians. When Kissinger pressed Dobrynin about truce violations, Dobrynin was unresponsive. When Kissinger warned that..."There should be no illusion that we will forget who put us in this uncomfortable position." Dobrynin's rejoinder was incisive: "In that case, you should go after Senator Fulbright!" But time was running out on the President, not on a Congress which had become embroiled in the politics of Watergate to the exclusion of all else. It was the United States Congress that finally "lost" the Vietnam War, neatly unraveling all the progress made in Vietnamization within a matter of months, first by denying the historical Presidential Prerogative of using American military power, then by denying a valiant ally the means to defend itself. With President Nixon's resignation in August of 1974, the death knell had sounded for South Vietnam.

.50 calibre machine gun incorporated into the "Fire Fly" system on a Nighthawk Huey. The battery of landing lights picked out targets, and the .50 knocked them out. (US Army via Wayne Mutza)

American crew which had just been shot down while on a training mission in a VNAF UH-1H rushes to a Huey of the 282nd AHC, I Corps area, 1972. (Mike Lecroy via Wayne Mutza)

SP-5 Ramiro Ramirez firing his "free 60" from a Huey during a mission with the 240th Assault Helicopter Company on 24 January, 1971. (US Army via Wayne Mutza)

Hughes OH-6A Loach (Cayuse, the official name, was never used by the troops) was the primary scout helicopter. It carried a pilot and gunner/crew chief who usually had, among other weapons, a free 60. The pilot controlled a minigun mounted on the left side of the fuselage. (US Army)

Army Huey crew being briefed by VNAF officer at Quang Tri Citadel in April, 1972, during the Easter Invasion. (F. C. Brown)

"Elusive Butterfly", an OH-6A Loach at Nha Be in 1971. (Wayne Mutza)

All Black Loach of 1 Cav, 1st Cav at Camp Bear Cat, 1971. (Wayne Mutza)

Another view of the OH-6A at Freedom Hill in 1971. Loach crews flew the most dangerous missions assigned to Army aviators in Vietnam. (F. C. Brown)

Loach cockpit...at Freedom Hill, Danang, 1971. (F. C. Brown)

Loaches flew low and usually slowly enough to get a good look at the ground. And they often paid the price. This Loach was shot down near Camp Bear Cat in 1971. (Wayne Mutza)

Sand-filled 55-gallon drums formed aircraft revetments at Freedom Hill for these Loaches. (F. C. Brown)

OH-58A Kiowa was an unpopular replacement for the Loach, most pilots complaining about its lack of power and poor directional control. This Kiowa is landing at Phu Cat on 3 August, 1971. (Norman E. Taylor)

(Below) OH-58A patrolling the coast on 25 March, 1971. It is armed with a minigun on the port side. (UPI via Bell)

"Murder Inc.", an AH-1G of the 20th Aerial Rocket Artillery, armed with 76-rocket package (XM-200 system). Its call sign was "Blue Max 33". (Wayne Mutza)

AH-1G, 69-16422, of Troop B, 7th Squadron, 1st Cav, at the rearm pad Kae Sanh, 19 February, 1971. (Mike Campbell)

AH-1G Cobra departing Phu Cat on a mission in support of the Republic of Korea "Tiger" Division, which was patrolling the nearby mountains in search of NVA, 20 April, 1971. (Norman E. Taylor)

(Left) Cobra crew at Phu Cat taking a break between missions, 20 April,1971. (Norman E. Taylor)

(Below) Neal Thompson's "Hammer Head", an AH-1G Cobra in which he killed an NVA tank. (See color painting.) It is fitted with engine heat-masking shrouds which became a necessity after the communists introduced the SA-7, a shoulder-fired heat-seeking missile. (Neal Thompson)

Cobra fitted with a magazine for the M-35 Armament subsystem, which utilized a 20mm Vulcan cannon. In this case it is armed with a 7-shot rocket pod.

1975—THE END

By the beginning of 1975 the North Vietnamese had eleven divisions in South Vietnam, with a 225,000-man force, plus 150,000 guerrillas and administrative troops. They were opposed by thirteen South Vietnamese divisions, which included just 180,000 main force ARVN (Regional and Popular Forces accounted for another 482,000 troops). Though the heavy rains of the monsoon had washed out many roads and bridges, the NVA had managed to push close enough to major population centers in South Vietnam to bring them under 130mm and 122mm artillery fire. As the dry season began in the south, the communists were in position to launch an all-out offensive. Their strategy, as always, was to attack selected targets where they enjoyed overwhelming numerical superiority. If successful, they would go after another target. If the United States did not retaliate with renewed bombing, the attacks would continue as long as they were successful. While numbers seemed to favor the South Vietnamese, they were in the disadvantageous position of having to defend large areas of territory. The North Vietnamese, with secure lines of supply which the cessation of US bombing had guaranteed, were able to concentrate their forces for attacks. On 6 January Phuoc Binh, the provincial capital of Phuoc Long Province, fell to the communists. For the first time in the war the South Vietnamese had lost an entire province. The loss of Phuoc Long Province, some scant 50 kilometers from Saigon, was like a dagger pointed at the heart of Thieu's government. It followed by a few weeks the meeting at which Thieu and his top military leaders had decided to consolidate their defenses by withdrawing from the central highlands.

The decision to withdraw from positions which would be difficult at best, and impossible at worst, to defend, was sound tactically. There was little more than territory to defend, since the majority of the population was located in the coastal cities and the delta of the south, and the coastal cities were thought to be defensible. Strategically, it was turned into a disaster by poor implementation. The commander of the Vietnamese Air Force (VNAF) was not even informed of this decision, and did not find out about it until his airplanes began the evacuation, under orders from the local military region commanders.

The communists began what would quickly turn into their final victorious assault on the night of 9 March, with an all-out attack on the central population center of Ban Me Thout. The NVA general Van Tien Dung had cleverly feinted towards Kontum and Pleiku, while building a five-to-one manpower advantage around Ban Me Thout covertly. The NVA fired more than 4,000 rounds of artillery into the city in advance of armor and infantry attacks, and by dawn one half of the city was in their hands. Though the VNAF tried to

provide close support, their A-37s could not survive in the environment created by AAA and SA-7 SAMs. Within a week the city had fallen, and despite orders from Thieu to defend it at all costs, the 23rd Division had fallen back after taking a severe beating.

In a meeting held at Cam Ranh Bay on 14 March, the South Vietnamese decided to withdraw from Pleiku and Kontum in order to conserve forces and build up for a counterattack on Ban Me Thout. The commander of military region II, Major General Phu, interpreted this to mean immediate evacuation of these two cities, and issued orders to that effect on the same day. The commander of the 6th Air Division of the VNAF was given forty-eight hours to evacuate Pleiku Airfield. He borrowed C-130s for the move and they began immediate shuttle flights into and out of the airport. This produced panic among the local population as well as the military, which turned its attention to the evacuation of their families instead of planning defense or counterattacks. It was the beginning of what would turn into a country-wide rout. The South Vietnamese decided to withdraw to Danang, the most defensible of the coastal cities, and the roads leading to Danang quickly became clogged with refugees and Regional and Popular Force troops. The airfield at Danang came under artillery fire, and the local VNAF commander was ordered to get all of his flyable aircraft out. In the confusion that followed this order, 180 aircraft were abandoned or lost to enemy fire and panicked ARVN troops, who overpowered VNAF security troops. The thousands of refugees pouring into the city made an effective defense impossible; on 29 March the communists marched into Danang virtually unopposed.

The communists now committed all of their reserves in an attempt to secure a military victory prior to the beginning of the rainy season. There would eventually be nineteen divisions, totalling some 325,000 regular army troops deployed in South Vietnam. The coastal cities fell in rapid order. There was mass confusion, with thousands of refugees attempting to flee southward in boats or by road. The communists shelled the columns of refugees continuously, killing more civilians than soldiers. The lack of centralized, cohesive leadership of ARVN began to tell, as one panicked unit after another fled southward, or attempted to leave the country. There were exceptions. Units of VNAF fought savagely at Phu Cat and Phan Rang. Pilots often loaded their own aircraft with bombs and fuel, as ground personnel assumed the responsibility for air base security after ARVN troops had fled. Before finally withdrawing to Tan Son Nhut, A-37 pilots were bombing so close to the airfield that "gear up" and "bombs away" were within minutes of each other. And not all of the units of ARVN collapsed without a

VNAF A-1H Skyraider loaded with 500-lb. bombs in its revetment at Bien Hoa prior to a 1971 mission. (Wayne Mutza)

fight. There were isolated instances of heroic resistance, including what was to become the climactic battle for South Vietnam—Xuan Loc.

By the time the battle for Xuan Loc began, all operational aircraft of the VNAF had been flown to Bien Hoa and Binh Thuy. The VNAF flew more than 600 sorties in support of ARVN in the battle. Unfortunately, most, if not all, of these were against well-defended NVA positions. The roads leading south were bumper-to-bumper with NVA trucks, tanks, and SAM missile carriers. These were targets which begged for interdiction, but which were ignored. Xuan Loc fell on April 22, with the chewed-up 18th Division falling back to Saigon. It had put up a valiant defense, but was overwhelmed by three NVA Divisions. The fate of South Vietnam was now sealed. Saigon was surrounded by 13 communist divisions, whose deadly accurate 130mm artillery could devastate the city.

President Thieu went on national television on April 21 to announce his resignation, denouncing the United States for abandoning South Vietnam. His resignation had come as a result of a communist demand, backed up with the threat of destruction of Saigon. In addition to their heavy artillery, the North Vietnamese were able to employ captured VNAF A-37s to bomb Tan Son Nhut, thereby bringing to a halt the fixed-wing evacuation of the capital. The only way out now was by helicopter, and President Ford ordered implementation of OPERATION FREQUENT WIND on 29 April. During its eighteen hours, FREQUENT WIND accounted for evacuation of 2,362 Americans, including the Fleet Marine Force which had been inserted for security purposes during the operation, and 6,422 non-Americans. American aircraft used during this operation included Marine H-53 and CH-46s, and USAF HH-53Bs, flown off of the USS Midway. It was the first time ever that USAF helicopters had operated from a carrier. The Navy helicopters operated from the USS Okinawa and USS Hancock. Several Air America Hueys played an impromptu role in the evacuation, as well. A total of 640 sorties were flown into the makeshift landing zones in and around Saigon during the evacuation, which began in darkness. They came under fire from both communist and ARVN AAA, and several SA-7 missiles were fired at the US helicopters. None were hit. Some NVA AAA sites were attacked by USAF F-4s, covering the evacuation from Utapao, and by Navy F-4s flying off the carriers Midway and Coral Sea. The F-14 flew its first combat missions in its first deployment aboard USS Enterprise, though no enemy fighters challenged the evacuation fleet, and no shots were fired by the Tomcats.

The US Seventh Fleet stood off the coast, ready to receive any survivors who could scramble to safety. Several VNAF pilots flew their helicopters out to the ships. Those who landed aboard helped to push their own aircraft off the overcrowded decks and into the South China Sea. Some abandoned their helicopters in mid-air when there was no longer room on the ships. In one case, a VNAF pilot landed aboard a US carrier in an O-1, with his entire

Pulling maintenance on an A-1 at Bien Hoa, 1971. After the Easter Invasion of 1972, it was obvious that the A-1s could not operate in the environment created by a newly equipped NVA, which carried devastatingly effective AAA. (Wayne Mutza)

family. Saigon's final agony was over. For days prior to the surrender on 30 April, there had been uncontrolled looting and panic. Nguyen Cao Ky's pleas to be allowed to fight on in the Mekong Delta were denied by American officials, and he too was forced to flee on the last day of the war, landing his helicopter on the Midway. It was crystal clear that America was irrevocably abandoning Vietnam. The sacrifices of blood and money poured into Vietnam throughout 16 years of direct American involvement were ignored by a US Congress which refused further aid to the South Vietnamese, and hamstrung the American President in his attempts to live up to a generation of promises. America's Vietnam War was over on 30 April, 1975, as communist tanks rumbled through the gates of an abandoned US Embassy in Saigon, soon to be renamed Ho Chi Minh City.

23rd Tactical Wing A-1 taxies out for a 1971 mission from Bien Hoa. (Wayne Mutza)

A-1E of the 23rd Tactical Wing at Bien Hoa in 1971. The Skyraiders became a maintenance nightmare after 1973, and most were put into flyable storage. (Wayne Mutza)

T-28D of the Royal Laotion Air Force.

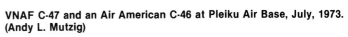

(Left) T-28 of the Cambodian Air Force at Phnom Penh in 1971. (Wayne Mutza)

VNAF C-47 and an Air American C-46 at Pleiku Air Base, July, 1973. (Andy L. Mutzig)

ESCAPE!

Pham Quang Khiem graduated from Technical High School in Saigon in 1966, then enrolled in the University of Saigon as an English Literature Major. He attended the language school at Lackland AFB, Texas, as a VNAF air cadet in 1969. He received his basic pilot training at Randolph AFB, then moved on to Keesler AFB, where he flew the T-28. Eventually, he was assigned to fly transport aircraft, and was pilot-in-command of C-123K aircraft before moving up to the C-130.

Khiem's family of 10 included 5 boys, all of them in the military during the war. Three of his brothers were in the VNAF, and his oldest brother was the chief training officer for the 62nd Wing of VNAF at Nha Trang, an A-37 unit. It was a family that believed in their country and was willing to fight to save it—almost to the bitter end.

1/Lt. Pham Quang Khiem was a C-130 co-pilot in the VNAF at the time of the collapse of South Vietnam. Through an extraordinary set of circumstances, and with a daring born of a realization of the probable outcome of the war, he was able to get his entire family out of South Vietnam just before the surrender. This is his story, in his own words:

We flew one of the last resupply missions into Danang, at 11 PM on the night before its loss. As soon as we landed and taxied to the ramp, an ARVN major jumped into the aircraft, through the crew door, to assure himself of a seat. I knew that the thousands of people in the terminal would rush the airplane after seeing this, so I kicked him off. I was only a First Lieutenant, but the aircraft commander, Captain Chuan, was searching the terminal building for his family. As it was, the ramp was filled with refugees almost immediately anyway. I had about 20,000 pounds of cargo on board, and I shouted at them to let me offload first, then I could take about 200 of them on board. Since we had no way to control this crowd, I told the Loadmaster not to open the crew door (in the nose), but to do all unloading and loading through the ramp at the rear of the airplane. As soon as the cargo was off, the panic was on! People rushed onto the airplane, and we couldn't do anything to stop them. As I looked out of the cockpit, I couldn't see anything but people. When we cranked the engines, they scattered, and we were able to taxi out.

The Loadmaster called on the intercom as we taxied, "Lieutenant, I cannot close the ramp because of the people on it!" I said, "Hang on!", then hit the brakes. That jammed them in tight enough to allow him to close the ramp. Just as we solved that problem, I looked up and saw the Wing Commander of the helicopter wing hovering in front of the airplane in his Huey. He wanted us to stop and load his family into the airplane, but since there was no possible place to put them, we just kept taxiing, and he broke away.

When we got to the end of the runway, I thought it was all over. There was an MP in a 2-1/2 ton truck loaded with his family, blocking the taxiway and pointing his M-16 into the cockpit. He motioned that he wanted us to load his family aboard. I nodded, but motioned for him to move the truck so we could line up on the runway before loading them. As soon as he backed up, we lined up and took off without hesitation! As soon as we got to our cruising altitude, I got out of my seat to take a look back in the cabin. It was an unbelievable sight! There were people hanging on the paratroop static line cables that run the length of the cabin, and no one was sitting down. When we off loaded at Tan Son Nhut, we did an actual head count of 350 people. That flight and the panic I saw in Danang got me to thinking. I thought, "If it ever looks like the same thing is going to happen in Saigon, I will take a C-130 and get my family out!"

By comparison, the evacuation of Pleiku had been orderly. It had taken place one week previous to the fall of Danang, and I had flown three missions into and out of Pleiku, evacuating the families of VNAF personnel. Unfortunately, the civil population of Pleiku learned of the evacuation and stormed the airport, forcing 5 C-130s enroute from Saigon to turn back before the airlift was complete. But that was our first taste of the panic which soon rolled over the entire country as the North Vietnamese advanced. Some of our C-130s flew bombing missions to destroy the aircraft left behind. They were loaded with 55-gallon drums of gasoline or napalm, then dropped them on VNAF aircraft abandoned on the ramps.

I flew missions to Nha Trang in that evacuation on the 31st of March. Then, on the 2nd of April I hitched a ride into Phan Rang on a C-130 "bladder bird", hoping to locate my younger brother, who was an airman in the headquarters there. I had hoped to take him back to Saigon to be with the rest of the family. I could not locate him though, and had to return to Saigon without him. (We were very lucky though...he showed up at my parents' home in Saigon five minutes

Pham Quang Khiem at the controls of a C-130.

before our escape!) On the flight back to Saigon, I thought to myself, "If Phan Rang is lost, it won't be long before communists are in Saigon." It was time to plan my escape.

As the situation deteriorated further, there was a lot of talk among the pilots of stealing a C-130 and getting their families out. I suspected that this was just talk, and though I was willing to do just that, I never said a word about it to anyone in my squadron. Headquarters must have considered the possibility of that happening though, because they ordered the airplanes to be fueled with only enough gas to accomplish their missions. If you were going to Phan Rang, they just gave you enough gas, plus a small reserve, to get there. You would have to refuel there in order to get back to Saigon. That was a problem in taking an airplane to get out of the country. Another problem was finding someone to help you. You might fool the Engineer and Loadmasters about what you were doing, but you wouldn't be able to fool another pilot.

One of my best friends in the VNAF was Major Nguyen Huu Canh, who was in our sister squadron (I was in the 435th, and he was in the 437th). We had been friends for a long time, and we discussed the possibility of getting out. I knew that once a pilot managed to steal an airplane and escape that the VNAF would tighten security and make further escapes impossible. I told him, "If we are not number one to escape, we will never be number two!" His family was in DaLat, and he wanted to get them to Saigon before leaving. On 2 April DaLat was overrun by the communists and he lost contact with them. After that he was then willing to go along with anything I planned. On 3 April all the C-130s were used on bombing missions. I needed to be number one standby on the mission planning board. But I needed time to tell my family what I had planned. I went to the Squadron Ops Officer and told him I didn't feel good, and he agreed to drop me to the bottom of the list. This gave me a chance to run home for lunch.

When I got home, I took my brother aside and told him what I had planned. I asked him to take charge of the family, which had all gathered in Saigon, and to keep them close to home. If they heard from me they were to go immediately to the Long Thanh airport, which was about seventeen miles southeast of Saigon. Long Thanh was a former US Army airbase, which I had landed on during training. It had been closed since the US withdrawal in 1973, and was deserted. I told them to rush there as soon as they heard from me. I didn't know how I was going to get an airplane, but I would try.

When I got back to the airport, I waited for something to happen. At three o'clock, just when I thought we wouldn't get out that day,

VNAF-operated T-41s in the trainer role. (Pham Quang Khiem)

my friend called to say that he had been assigned to a food resupply mission to Phan Rang. Actually, one of the other pilots had been assigned to the mission, but when he complained that he had already flown two missions that day and was tired, my friend volunteered to take his place. I ran home (my home was within a mile of the airport) and told my family to leave for Long Dien immediately. There was still another problem. Since we were in different squadrons, we would not ordinarily fly together. In fact, I could not even get into his squadron area, since the guards did not know me and I had no pass to get in. Once again we were lucky. The airplane he was supposed to take had mechanical problems, and his squadron borrowed one of our airplanes. I met him at the airplane. Now the problem was going to be to get rid of his co-pilot. His co-pilot had gone to get something to eat, and when he came back I told him that I would be glad to take his place in order to fly with my friend, and to look for my missing brother. He was only too happy to take the rest of the day off, especially since he had a date! I warned him not to go back to the squadron, since they might not like our switching places without authorization. The flight engineer and loadmasters accepted the story without too many questions, since I knew them both.

These missions had become so routine that we could take off within a few minutes, and that created another problem for my plan. The seventeen miles from Saigon to Long Thanh was on a rough country road, and I knew my family could not get there before 4 PM. I also knew that once we took off, timing would be essential. We couldn't land at Long Thanh and wait around for them to show up. A C-130 landing on an abandoned airstrip would raise an alarm, and besides, the rest of the crew would know right away what we were doing. I had to delay our takeoff somehow, so I made sure that I got to the airplane before the Flight Engineer. I pulled several circuit breakers, and since they were breakers that would normally not pop by themselves, I knew they would be hard to spot. One of them was for the APU starter, and that caused a delay right away. The FE finally spotted the popped breakers though, and we cranked the engines at 3:30. Our procedures were strictly by the book on this flight, and I am sure the crew was wondering what had gotten into the pilot, since each checklist was being read agonizingly thoroughly. They probably figured their new co-pilot (me) was making sure things went smoothly with an unfamiliar crew. I delayed as long as I could, but we were still rolling before 4 PM.

In all my calculations about where we would go, the problem of fuel had always been uppermost in my mind. I did not think we would have more than an hour-and-a-half of fuel on board, which would only have been enough to get us to Thailand, and that was not far enough to insure our safety. Getting this airplane though was an opportunity we could not pass up, no matter what the outcome. The first thing I did when I got out to the airplane was flip the master switch on to check the fuel level. My heart leapt into my throat when I saw that

the tanks were full! The line crewman must have anticipated my surprise, because he apologized, explaining that he had taken a smoke break while fuelling the airplane, and forgot about the new rule regarding rationing. He begged me not to turn him in! Of course, I gave him a stern look and told him not to let it happen again, and then told him to forget about it. With a full load of fuel we could fly all the way to Singapore. This was my first choice because I had heard that they needed pilots in Singapore, and maybe they could use me! My friend was still despondent about the loss of his family, and he didn't care where we went as long as it was out of the country. He said, "Once we are airborne, it's your show."

We had filed an IFR flight plan, but I did not call for a clearance when we taxied out. The crew knew we were going to Phan Rang though, so when we turned southeast instead of northeast, they would know something was wrong. Right after takeoff, I turned off all the radios and the transponder*. Then I turned to the pilot, and said on intercom, "What's the matter with them anyway? Why are they sending us to Long Thanh to pick up those people?" Now the crew knew that we were going to Long Thanh, but they thought that we had been sent there by headquarters. We were at 2,000 feet, and my friend was eager to get to Long Thanh. I told him to slow down. "If we fly slow, maybe they will think it is a helicopter, or an O-1 on their radar screens."

It didn't take us long to get there anyway, and as we began a slow circle to the right, I looked down and tried to spot my family. The place was deserted, and I got a sinking feeling. The next time around, I searched the country road for a sign of them. There they were! Five little cars, about half a mile from the airport! I turned to my friend and told him to go ahead and land. I knew that my brother had briefed the family to run onto the airplane as soon as they saw the ramp come down. As soon as we landed, I saw their cars pull onto the end of the runway. We taxied to the turnaround and I asked the Loadmaster to open the ramp. When he had it open, I asked him to offload the cargo, which was 20,000 pounds of rice. So far they didn't suspect anything, but I knew that I could not take them out of the country without letting them know what I was doing. As soon as my family was on board, I said, "Gentlemen, I have to tell you that this aircraft will not go back to Saigon anymore. We are leaving the country! Anyone who does not want to go is free to leave now." The Flight Engineer unhooked his seatbelt and headset and got halfway out of his seat, then sat back down and said he would go with us. The number one Loadmaster must have thought we were defecting to the North Vietnamese. He was a ten-year VNAF veteran, and he got off the airplane as quickly as he could. The other Loadmaster was on his first C-130 ride, and didn't know what was going on—he just stood by the open ramp.

*Author's note: The transponder is a piece of avionics equipment which can be set to a specified four-number code, which will read out onto a controller's radar screen, positively identifying the aircraft. Turning the transponder off gave them a measure of anonymity.

C-130A of VNAF being loaded with supplies prior to a 1975 mission. (Pham Quang Khiem)

Khiem poses with one of the members of his family who escaped with him to Singapore. (Pham Quang Khiem)

As we started taxiing to the takeoff end of the runway, I saw our Loadmaster talking to several ARVN soldiers who had shown up in a Jeep. Our landing had aroused their curiosity. The Loadmaster was gesturing wildly, so I knew he was telling them our plan. As we turned to take off, the Jeep pulled alongside and they pointed an M-79 grenade launcher at the cockpit. But I didn't think they would fire, and we started the takeoff. Our ramp was still open though, and I had to run back to start it coming up. I grabbed the confused new Loadmaster and told him to hold the switch until the ramp was up, then ran back to the cockpit. I got back into my seat just in time to raise the gear for Major Canh. From the time we landed until we took off again seemed like a long time, but it was only seven minutes.

Once we were off, we headed out to sea at tree-top level. Once we got out over the sea, we dropped down to sea level. I mean, we were low! Later, my family would say that they thought they were getting out by boat, we were so low! It was extremely humid in the rear, so much so, in fact, that a fog formed which was so thick that they could not see each other. After an hour of skimming the wave tops we climbed to 16,000 feet and we set a course directly for Singapore. I got on the PA system and announced that we were now over international waters. There was a very joyous cheer from the cabin. The Flight Engineer then told me that he had planned to do exactly what we were doing, with another pilot in the Squadron. He had been into the Singapore airport several times, and briefed us on its layout. The Loadmaster had no family in South Vietnam, and was just happy to be getting out alive.

We arrived in Singapore at 7 PM. It was dark and raining when I called Approach Control for instructions. I couldn't understand their reply, so I just changed to Tower Frequency, and called, "Singapore Tower, Herky 460. Request landing instruction." They replied, "Herky 460, cleared to land runway 02." They gave me the wind and altimeter setting, but didn't ask, "Who are you?" or "What the hell

Cessna U-17As of VNAF based at Tan Son Nhut AB. They were used for liason and psychological warfare. (Norman E. Taylor)

are you doing here?" So we just went in and landed on 02! This was the civilian international airport and I thought that they would get excited when a military aircraft landed there. But when we parked on the ramp, the ground personnel came and hooked up an auxilliary power cart when the engines were shut down, then left. I told my people that they were now in a free country, but that no one was allowed to leave the aircraft until we had surrendered to the proper authorities.

My friend, my brother and I all changed into our civilian clothes, got off the airplane, and headed for the terminal building. It took us a half hour to find the airport office. When I explained to the guard on duty that we were a group of Vietnamese who had just gotten out of the country, and that we wanted to talk to his boss, he said, "Well, the airport office closes at 5 PM. Why don't you guys come back at eight tomorrow morning?" We finally convinced him that we had entered his country illegally, and that he had to do something about it. Well, he couldn't find his boss, who was out partying somewhere. We wandered around the airport until midnight, then went back out to the airplane. I found that my people were well taken care of. Some of the ground crew from the airlines had become curious, and had come over to our airplane. When they found 56 refugees from the war, they brought food and drink from the airline service area.

Finally, at about 1 AM, twenty trucks filled with police surrounded our airplane, and we surrendered to the Chief of Police. We explained that we would like political asylum in Singapore, but that if they could not take us, we would like the gas to get to Australia or New Zealand. They called the Vietnamese counsel, and he came down to the airport. We told him that we did not want to go back to Vietnam, and that we wanted asylum. He left without commenting, and we never heard from him again. The local officials could not make up their minds what to do with us. It was obvious that we had created a problem that they did not want to deal with. (It was a problem they had not had before.) Finally, I suggested that they just give us the gas and the charts to get to Australia and we would leave. That seemed like a good idea to them, since the only person who seemed to have the authority to OK political asylum was the Prime Minister, and he was out of the country for two weeks.

RF-5A taxies out for a long recce mission, Bien Hoa, December, 1971. (Wayne Mutza)

F-5B of VNAF 23rd Tactical Wing taxies at Bien Hoa, 1971. The F-5 was the first jet operated in strength by VNAF. The first units were equipped in early 1967 and eventually 8 squadrons of F-5s were operated by VNAF. (Wayne Mutza)

F-5A at Bien Hoa in 1971. (Wayne Mutza)

This RF-5A of the 23rd Tactical Wing suffered a near-miss by a Chicom 122mm rocket at Bien Hoa, December, 1972. (Wayne Mutza)

A pair of VNAF U-6 Otters formate over the Mekong. They were used for psychological warfare and intelligence gathering. (USAF)

VNAF CH-47 Chinook enroute to a fire base north of Bien Hoa. VNAF began operating the Chinook as the US Army began to withdraw. (USAF)

We were deciding how to get to Australia when the matter of how we would pay for the gas came up. They would not accept anything but US currency, and even after taking up a collection among the passengers, we only had about 400 dollars of the 5,000 we needed to pay for the fuel. We had another couple of thousand dollars in gold watches, rings, and jewelry, but when I asked the airport authorities if they could accept them, they said, "No way! We don't take that junk—US dollars only!" "Well," I said, "If I don't have fuel, I can't go anywhere." Fortunately, they were sympathetic. We did create a problem for them, but they must have had an idea of how the war would end. They billeted us in the local jail until the end came, then treated us as heroes. Within three weeks we were on our way to a new life in the United States.

Khiem had managed to get his entire family out, with the exception of his youngest brother, who was in the Army, stationed at Vung Tau. The original plan called for an escape attempt on 6 April, when the family expected him to be home. But the opportunity that presented itself was too good to pass up, and he was left behind. After the communists took over, he was sent to a reeducation camp for two years of brainwashing. He is back in Saigon, and the family would like to bring him to the United States, but they don't know how. Major Nguyen Huu Canh is presently flying for an oil drilling company in Houston. Khiem has flown for several air charter companies in the United States, amassing a total of over 6,300 hours while earning his Airline Transport Pilot rating. Of the thousands of former VNAF pilots who have settled in the US, only six fixed-wing pilots are still flying for a living.

O-1 Bird Dogs of the 23rd Tactical Wing. Though VNAF operated large numbers of FAC aircraft, the pilots were never trained as well as their US counterparts, did not have the authority to direct air strikes, and were often the least skilled pilots in their respective units. (USAF and Wayne Mutza)

VNAF UH-1H at Danang, 1971. (F. C. Brown)

VNAF H-34 at Danang, September, 1971. The H-34 was among the first helicopters operated by VNAF, and was gradually replaced by the Huey as the US withdrew. (USAF)

WHAT THEY LEFT BEHIND

At the end of the battle of Xuan Loc, it was estimated that the VNAF still had 1,492 aircraft, making it the third largest air force in the world (135 of these were "redlined"). As the fabric of discipline within the armed forces began to unravel, individual pilots used some of the aircraft to escape. There was no comprehensive plan to evacuate aircraft to prevent them falling into the hands of the communists. Attempts were made to destroy the 380-plus aircraft left at air bases further north as the retreat south progressed. In the confusion of that retreat, it is impossible to make an accurate accounting of exactly how many of these aircraft were destroyed, and how many were captured. 1983 estimates of US aircraft in possession of the Vietnamese include 15 F-5As, 25 A-37Bs, 4 C-130s, 10 CH-47s, and 45 UH-1s, though it is acknowledged that many of these would be inoperable because of a lack of spares.

During the collapse, 27 of 87 F-5s were flown out to Thailand, while only 8 of 95 A-37s managed to get out. 11 of the 26 flyable A-1s were flown to Utapao, while 13 of 38 C-47s landed in Thailand crammed with refugees. Unfortunately, many of the C-47s abandoned were gunship versions with forward-looking infrared equipment. Only 6 of 23 C-130s made it out, and just 3 of the 37 AC-119s got out; 8 C-119 transports were also left behind. 5 of 33 C-7s reached Thailand. 114 O-1s were abandoned, and only 30 of the 434 UH-1s in VNAF inventory were used in the evacuation. 32 CH-47s were left behind, as were 72 other aircraft, including T-41s, U-6s, O-2s, and U-17s.

The F-5s lost to the communists included 5 of the newer E models, which were equipped with the Emerson Electric APQ-153 radar. They also had radar bombing beacons, and early versions of the AIM-9 Sidewinder AAMs. All South Vietnamese gunships captured were equipped with the M-39 20mm Gatling gun. None of the equipment contained in the captured aircraft was considered "sensitive" by the US.

O-1 at Phu Cat on 11 May, 1971. (Norman E. Taylor)

DeHavilland C-7 Caribou operated by Air America, the CIA Airline. At Cheo Reo, south of Pleiku, April, 1972. (Andy L. Mutzig)

VNAF C-123K at Bien Hoa, December, 1971. The Provider was another USAF aircraft that was passed on to VNAF when the US withdrawal began. (Wayne Mutza)

VNAF U-17 equipped for leaflet drops. (USAF)

(Left) Air America C-7 Caribou in the distinctive Blue and White livery of the CIA airline and its subsidiary.

The largest transport operated by VNAF was the C-130A. (Pham Quang Kheim)

EPILOG

On the 10th anniversary of the signing of the Paris Peace Accords, several network news programs devoted time to looking back at the events surrounding the "end of the war". These were superficial reminiscences, concentrating for the most part on the national binge of maudlin emotion which accompanied the homecoming of the POWs. Very little was said about the 2500 unaccounted-for men, some of whom may very well still be prisoners of the North Vietnamese today. And practically nothing was said about events which transpired after the US pullout. The major media was not ready to acknowledge their bias, nor their patently inaccurate reportage of the war, even 10 years later. There is no doubt that press coverage of the Vietnam War was slanted. And, while it is true that that is most often the case in time of war, it is also usual for a nation's press to err on the side of the nation. Why the press of the United States turned against the leadership of the nation on this issue is still not completely clear. It might be ascribed to one of those periodic glitches in the national psyche which cause aberrant behavior. Norman Podhoretz, in his book, "Why We Were in Vietnam" (Simon & Schuster, 1982), ascribed the altogether irrational behavior of American liberals as reverse McCarthyism. The liberal community's bitter, and more often than not, inaccurate, attacks on US Vietnam policy could not be ascribed to thoughtful reflection.

Certainly, there can be no doubt in anyone's mind about the motives of the North Vietnamese communists. They claimed throughout the war that they did not have any troops in the south—that they were in fact only lending moral support to their communist brethren in the south, and that the war was a civil war. But the final outcome gives the lie to all of their posturing for world opinion. They fed their southern brethren into the meat grinder that was the Tet Offensive of 1968, and when the Viet Cong had ceased to be a viable force, the North Vietnamese took over the war. When victory came in 1975, what was left of the southern communist nationalist movement—Viet Cong, National Liberation Front, Provisional Revolutionary Government—was quickly disbanded. Non-communist members, or those who demonstrated an unwillingness to shoulder the mantle of North Vietnamese sovereignty, were arrested and either executed or sent to re-education camps. As if to underscore their disdain for the fiction of southern socialist independence, the North Vietnamese renamed Saigon "Ho Chi Minh City".

Those in the Viet Cong who survived the initial re-education process, and who later managed to escape, described life under their North Vietnamese masters. Nguyen Cong Hoan, an NLF agent who surfaced to become a member of the post-1975 government, and who fled the country in 1977, acknowledged that the North Vietnamese had executed "tens of thousands" in the provinces, and that the people of the south now knew "the most inhuman and oppressive regime they have ever known." Truong Nhu Tang, the former Minister of Justice of the PRG, got out in 1979. His opinion of the North Vietnamese rule was: "Never has any previous regime brought such masses of people to such desperation. Not the military dictators, not the colonialists, not even the ancient Chinese overlords."

The North Vietnamese quickly adopted Soviet methods of controlling the population. All books which had been published during previous regimes were burned, as were most philosophical works, including the work of such diverse authors as Sartre and Carnegie. Prior to the NVA takeover, there had been twenty-seven daily newspapers, three television stations, and twenty radio stations. They may not have been hotbeds of dissent in the American manner, but freedom of the press was observed by the Thieu government. Under communist rule, there are two newspapers, one TV station, and two radio stations.

Buddhist demonstrations during the Diem rule had received worldwide attention, and when a monk immolated himself pictures were flashed around the world. But when twelve monks and nuns immolated themselves in 1975 to protest the new communist regime, the press of the world all but ignored their protest. According to Thich Manh Giac, a Buddhist who escaped, the communists "arrested hundreds of monks, confiscated hundreds of pagodas and converted them to government administration buildings, removed and smashed Buddha and Bodhisattva statues, prohibited celebration of the Buddha's birthday as a national holiday, and forbade monks to travel and preach by ordering restrictions in the name of national security." The monks were not the only ones forbidden travel rights. All Vietnamese are required to carry internal passports for travel within the country, and many thousands

An example of the destructive accuracy of close air support. This hill in the the highlands was the site of an NVA outpost. (Norman E. Taylor)

OV-10 Nail FACs provided on-site command and control during the Mayaguez rescue. (USAF)

C-7A in flight over the central highlands. (USAF)

have been moved to new "economic zones", a communist euphemism for rural concentration camps, where they are forced to clear land and dig canals in order to eke out a meager living. Medical care is reserved for communist cadres. Thousands have committed suicide, and thousands more have fled the country in boats that were anything but sea-worthy, in effect choosing the one chance in ten of survival at sea over a life in one of the most brutal totalitarian states in history.

The liberal ideal seems to be a socialist state which is utopian in its egalitarian treatment of the population. Vietnam has never been a shining example of this dream, and the communist victory in 1975 has done nothing to improve the Vietnamese standard of living. Indeed, the common man was demonstrably better off under the authoritarian regime of Thieu than he is under the totalitarian state run by the North Vietnamese. Per-capita income in South Vietnam has slipped to sixty-three percent of what it was in 1976. War is one of the few activities run well by a totalitarian state, and Vietnam is no exception. The end of the Vietnam War was not the end at all. Khymer rebels still harass the occupation forces of North Vietnam in Kampuchea (formerly known as Cambodia), and Laos demands a large army of occupation to control its peoples. The communist regime of Vietnam maintains a 180,000-man army in Cambodia, diverting scarce resources which could be used to build a peacetime economy. Fully fifty percent of its GNP is devoted to war. Economic growth is near zero.

Saigon Harbor from 2500 feet in July of 1971. (Norman E. Taylor)

And of course there is the South, with its ubiquitous corruption and a population which had become accustomed to freedom. The peasants, lacking incentive to produce more food than they need to survive, have reduced the rice harvest; food production fell by 230,000 tons in 1981. Inflation is 100 percent annually, and the black market thrives. A 12-ounce can of Coke sells for $8.00, and a tube of toothpaste, $24.50. Under the South Vietnamese government of Thieu, a typical government worker made 25,000 piastres a month, and was able to buy a kilogram of meat for 50 piastres. Under the North Vietnamese, the same worker makes 100 dong a month, and will pay all of that for the same kilogram of meat.

The International Monetary Fund has refused to approve further economic aid to Vietnam until they provide evidence of economic reforms. But Vietnam is ill-suited to reform, economic or social, and they will continue to pile up bad debts as long as countries continue to lend them money. In this regard, Vietnam has become somewhat of an albatross around the Soviet neck. They unquestionably control Indochina, but the price they are paying amounts to two billion dollars a year.

Vietnam is unquestionably another example of the failure of socialism to provide even an adequate existence for its people. But it is more than that. It has become a sorrowful footnote to a page in American history. That great humanitarian instinct which led four American Presidents to send aid to a small democratic nation which was struggling for survival against a totalitarian aggressor was repudiated by a neo-isolationist Congress. Millions of Indochinese have died as a result of the American pullout. Millions more suffer under one of the most inhuman regimes in history. Americans have begun to deal with the American involvement in Vietnam. American liberals, represented by Jimmy Carter, who in 1977 called American Vietnam involvement a result of policies of "intellectual and moral poverty", were still blind

The heart of downtown Saigon, with its tightly-packed residences right up against the business district and modern hotels. (Norman E. Taylor)

to what their advocacy had wrought. President Reagan's assessment of America's Vietnam War seems much more accurate, given the ongoing travail of the peoples of Indochina. He has called American involvement a "noble cause".

Air America C-46 was pressed into the service of the International Control Commission after the peace agreements were signed. The yellow markings were to identify it as non-belligerent to ground forces, but North Vietnamese violations of the agreements began almost immediately, and these aircraft were no safer than those of the VNAF. (US Army)

Air America C-46 at Korat in 1974. (Bob Baldo)

Ubon Air Base at the height of LINEBACKER operations in September, 1972. (USAF)

C-119G of VNAFs 413th Transport Squadron at Tan Son Nhut, 17 July, 1971. This aircraft was later destroyed by Viet Cong rockets. (Norman E. Taylor)

VNAF C-119s at Pleiku (Left) and Bien Hoa (Below). (Wayne Mutza)

VNAF A-37s of the 524th Fighter Squadron, 62nd Wing, at Nha Trang. The A-37 was effective in the relatively permissive environment of South Vietnam prior to the Easter Invasion of 1972. After that, NVA units were equipped with anti-aircraft weaponry which made it almost impossible for the A-37 to operate effectively. (Norman E. Taylor and USAF)

North Vietnamese MiG-17 in earth revetment protected hardstand. The MiG-17 was the primary interceptor of the North Vietnamese. (Koku Fan)

(Below) NVA MiG-17 firing its 23mm cannon. (Koku Fan)

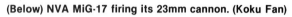

(Above) The North Vietnamese also operated the MiG-21, but in fewer numbers. (Koku Fan)

(Below) Much of the aerial reconnaissance carried out over the North in heavily defended areas was done by remotely piloted vehicles (RPVs). This Ryan Firebee was shot down by the communists, who staged this shot for the photographer. (Koku Fan)

THE MAYAGUEZ RESCUE MISSION

The final combat missions of the Vietnam War were flown in support of the rescue of the SS Mayaguez and its crew. While Congress would not allow President Ford to come to the aid of South Vietnam, the War Powers Act did not preclude his use of force to react to piracy on the high seas. And he reacted with a vengeance when Khymer Rouge gunboats seized the Mayaguez in international waters off the coast of Cambodia. Mayaguez had been steaming in the Gulf of Thailand, 60 miles southwest of Cambodia on 12 May, 1975, when it was stopped.

After the communists boarded and took command of Mayaguez, they steamed to Koh Tang Island. A US Navy P-3 Orion patrol aircraft kept track of the ship's movements during this short voyage. The following day surveillance was taken over by USAF F-111s, and later, AC-130s, which were able to monitor all activity, night and day, through the use of their LLTV and IR sensors. The AC-130s were fired on by communist guns on the island, and by the gunboats, but took no hits. Out of concern for the Mayaguez crew, they did not return the fire. The AC-130s were relieved during the day by A-7s and F-111s, which were ordered to fire warning shots across the bows of any Cambodian gunboats which attempted to leave Koh Tang. Three gunboats were sunk when they attempted to leave the island. The one boat which did manage to get to the mainland was the boat which carried the crew of Mayaguez.

After all attempts at a diplomatic solution had been exhausted, military forces were ordered to seize the Mayaguez and capture Koh Tang Island, releasing any crew still being held. The initial assault involved use of 230 Marines, divided between eleven USAF CH and HH-53 helicopters. The Marines were divided into: a boarding party, which was delivered to destroyer escort Harold E. Holt, which would come alongside Mayaguez and deliver the boarding party; and two beach assault forces, one each for western and eastern beaches.

Since it was not known whether any of the crew members were being held on the island, the beaches were not prepped with air strikes or artillery prior to the assault. Tactical aircraft orbited overhead, prepared to provide close air support should it become necessary. And it did become necessary. The communists had occupied the island in strength, and had both landing beaches well covered with small arms, rocket launchers, and mortars. One of the first two helicopters to offload Marines was so riddled with fire that it had to ditch in the ocean a mile from the beach. Both helicopters that assaulted the other beach were shot down by the intense groundfire. One of the Marine FACs survived the shoot-down and, as he swam away from the beach, began to call in air strikes by A-7s. He was joined in directing strafing runs by the co-pilot of the other downed HH-53, who had made it to the safety of the treeline on the beach in the company of several Marines. American losses after this first assault were four of five helicopters shot down and a fifth badly damaged. 14 Americans were dead, for unknown enemy losses. The beaches were far from secure, and the whereabouts of the Mayaguez crew was unknown. A rescue attempt by another HH-53 resulted in another shot-up helicopter. The situation on the ground was muddled enough to prevent massive application of airpower to silence the Cambodian gun positions. The only success in the operation so far had been the boarding of an abandoned Mayaguez, which was taken in tow by the Holt.

While furious fire-fights were taking place on the beaches, the Cambodians had decided to release the crew of the Mayaguez, which was being held on the Cambodian mainland. They put them aboard a Thai fishing boat, which delivered them under a white flag to the the US fleet. The recovery of the Mayaguez crew meant a freer hand for the air support aircraft. This was immediately taken advantage of by an orbiting AC-130 which quickly identified the friendly positions and brought enemy positions under fire with its 20, 40, and 105mm guns. More Marines were inserted on the beaches, bringing the total landing force to 131 Marines and 5 USAF crew members.

Once the crew of the Mayaguez had been released, it was decided to withdraw from Koh Tang. This turned out to be tougher than expected. The 200 defenders of the Island were well dug in with heavy weapons, and were fanatic in their attempts to shoot down the rescue aircraft. The USS Coral Sea steamed into the area, and would act as the collection point for the Marine assault forces as they were recovered from Koh Tang. The three remaining operational H-53s braved intense and accurate ground fire from the island to make the recovery, much of it after dark. All of the USAF crewmen demonstrated uncommon skill and coolness under fire. In spite of the fierce resistance of the Cambodians, no Americans were killed after the initial assault attempt. The final casualty count was 15 KIA, 3 MIA, and 50 WIA. A further 23 were killed in the crash of an Air Force H-53 prior to the start of the operation.

The rescue of the Mayaguez was loudly criticized by liberal members of Congress, who maintained that the operation had been ineptly managed. The communists evidently assessed it somewhat differently. Though the seizure of the Mayaguez was initiated by local Cambodian officials, without the knowledge or assent of the communist government in Phnom Penh, the quick and violent reaction of the United States demonstrated that—in the future, at least—America might be expected to be disinclined to negotiate Pueblo-type seizures.